Dappled Beauty

Dappled Beauty

*Through Lent with
Gerard Manley Hopkins*

Carys Walsh

CANTERBURY
PRESS

© Carys Walsh 2025
First published in 2025 by the Canterbury Press Norwich

Editorial office
3rd Floor, Invicta House
110 Golden Lane,
London EC1Y 0TG, UK
www.canterburypress.co.uk

Canterbury Press is an imprint of Hymns Ancient & Modern Ltd
(a registered charity)

Hymns Ancient & Modern® is a registered trademark of
Hymns Ancient & Modern Ltd
13A Hellesdon Park Road, Norwich,
Norfolk NR6 5DR, UK

All rights reserved. No part of this publication may be reproduced,
stored in a retrieval system, or transmitted,
in any form or by any means, electronic, mechanical,
photocopying or otherwise, without the prior permission of
the publisher, Canterbury Press.

Carys Walsh has asserted her right under the Copyright, Designs and
Patents Act 1988 to be identified as the Author of this Work

British Library Cataloguing in Publication data

A catalogue record for this book is available
from the British Library

ISBN: 978-1-78622-527-6

EU GPSR Authorised Representative
LOGOS EUROPE, 9 rue Nicolas Poussin, 17000, LA ROCHELLE, France
E-mail: Contact@logoseurope.eu

No part of this book may be used or reproduced in any manner for the purpose
of training artificial intelligence technologies or systems.

Typeset by Regent Typesetting

Contents

Introduction		1
Day 1	Ash Wednesday: 'Pied Beauty'	5
Day 2	Thursday: 'Inversnaid'	9
Day 3	Friday: 'Peace'	13
Day 4	Saturday: 'Moonrise June 19 1876'	17
Day 5	Monday: 'Hope Holds to Christ'	21
Day 6	Tuesday: 'Carrion Comfort'	26
Day 7	Wednesday: 'Heaven-Haven'	31
Day 8	Thursday: 'The Lantern Out of Doors'	34
Day 9	Friday: 'The Candle Indoors'	38
Day 10	Saturday: 'God's Grandeur'	42
Day 11	Monday: 'In the Valley of the Elwy'	47
Day 12	Tuesday: 'I Wake and Feel'	51
Day 13	Wednesday: 'Patience, Hard Thing'	55
Day 14	Thursday: 'My own heart let me more have pity on'	59
Day 15	Friday: 'The Wreck of the Deutschland' (1)	64
Day 16	Saturday: 'The Wreck of the Deutschland' (2)	69
Day 17	Monday: 'The Windhover'	74
Day 18	Tuesday: 'Hurrahing in Harvest'	79
Day 19	Wednesday: 'Felix Randal'	83

Day 20	Thursday: 'As Kingfishers Catch Fire'	87
Day 21	Friday: 'The Handsome Heart'	91
Day 22	Saturday: 'The Habit of Perfection'	95
Day 23	Monday: 'Justus Quidem (Thou art indeed just, Lord)'	100
Day 24	Tuesday: 'The Leaden Echo'	104
Day 25	Wednesday: 'The Golden Echo'	108
Day 26	Thursday: 'Thee, God, I come from, to thee go'	113
Day 27	Friday: 'Spring and Fall'	118
Day 28	Saturday: 'Binsey Poplars'	122
Day 29	Monday: 'The Caged Skylark'	127
Day 30	Tuesday: 'Let me be to Thee'	131
Day 31	Wednesday: 'The Sea and the Skylark'	135
Day 32	Thursday: 'Spring'	139
Day 33	Friday: 'Ribblesdale'	143
Day 34	Saturday: 'Repeat That, Repeat'	147
Day 35	Monday: 'To Seem the Stranger'	149
Day 36	Tuesday: 'No Worst'	153
Day 37	Wednesday: 'The Starlight Night'	157
Day 38	Maundy Thursday: 'Spelt from Sibyl's Leaves'	161
Day 39	Good Friday: 'The times are nightfall, look, their light grows less'	166
Day 40	Holy Saturday: 'That Nature Is a Heraclitean Fire and of the Comfort of the Resurrection'	170
Day 41	Easter Day: 'The Wreck of the Deutschland' (3)	175

Notes 179
References 184

Introduction

Entering Lent with Gerard Manley Hopkins

Lent is a time of drawing closer to Christ as we travel with him through his 40 wilderness days towards the Passion. We may enter this time in a spirit of preparation and penitence, hopeful of encountering Christ more deeply and fully; and along the way, we may be transformed as we discover what it means to bring the whole of ourselves before God in all our dappled existence.

Gerard Manley Hopkins, a poet who understood profoundly the dappled nature of God's world and humanity within it, is a rich companion for this season. A poet of breathtaking intensity and creativity, and with a 'love for subtlety and uncommonness',[1] he has gifted us flashing glimpses of God in the world in some of his most well-known poems, such as 'God's Grandeur', 'The Windhover' and 'Pied Beauty'. Born in London in 1844, he entered the Jesuit order as a young man and, already a writer of poetry, wrestled with how his poetic gift related to his priestly calling – and so he fell silent for several years. His return to writing, while studying at St Beuno's College in North Wales, birthed groundbreaking verse that sang of God's presence and shaped the craft of future poets. As the years turned and Hopkins left St Beuno's, he encountered times of personal darkness and turmoil. He moved frequently to new posts, often living in industrial places he found 'wretched' and which left him 'museless'.[2] He experienced times of profound desolation in the final few years of his life living as an academic and teacher in Dublin. When he died as a still-young man in

1889, he left for us a body of poetry with an imprint of struggle and rawness as indelible as his faith and love for the God he dedicated his life to praising.

It was only a few years ago that I began delving deeply into his poetry. Getting to know him and his work (and there is still much more to discover) has been a breathtaking experience of being moved, challenged and changed by a poet of intense faith and authenticity. Hopkins' poetic gift blends the vision of a seer with a vibrant creative craftsmanship and an understanding of the contours of the human heart in all its struggles and on its journey of faith. It is this variegated gift that makes Hopkins such a rich companion for the season of Lent.

Bringing the whole of ourselves to God

The 41 reflections in this collection of Hopkins' poems, one for each day of Lent (apart from Sundays) and taking us into Easter, include many of his most well-known verses; but it is a very personal choice of verse that has stirred and engaged me. Some of the poems speak directly to the season of Lent; some open out more generally a vision of God-with-us or linger over what it means to be human in a world shot through with glory and darkness. Some offer a glimpse of profound suffering and some ponder challenges of the Christian life. The poetic mood may change from day to day but, in the final week, the poetry will echo the shape and tone of Holy Week. I hope that, together, these poems share a vision of what it means to bring the whole of ourselves to God: in all our wildernesses, our temptations, our battles with self and faith, our desire to surrender and not surrender, our joy and our love of this muddled world and our apprehension of God's vivid presence at the heart of it.

INTRODUCTION

Reading Hopkins' poetry

As with so much poetry, the challenge in reading Hopkins' work is to resist the desire to 'master' it; the encouragement instead is to surrender to it, linger over it, and allow its heart-opening, challenging and sometimes playful language to do its work. Hopkins himself wrote to his friend Robert Bridges (whom we can thank for first publishing Hopkins' work in 1918, long after the poet's death) that he felt his poetry was 'made for performance, and that its performance is not reading with the eye, but loud, leisurely, poetical (not rhetorical), recitation, with long rests, long dwells on the rhyme and other marked syllables'.[3]

If this tells us something about reading his work, it also tells us a little about Hopkins' creative spirit, with his love of soundscapes, meaning-breaking language, and bounding, bouncing verse, which he called 'sprung rhythm'. As the reflections unfold, we shall encounter many examples of his soundscapes, his 'sprung rhythm' and other peculiarly 'Hopkins-esque' features of his writing. We shall also take the opportunity, with each reflection, to linger a little over Hopkins' life and faith, and reflect on how his poetry might speak beyond its words.

Along the way, we may also find ourselves challenged by his verse; we may be left pondering or wondering, tussling or praising. We may find ourselves resonating deeply with this poetry born out of a heart turned towards God; and with Hopkins, we may discover more of what it means to surrender the depths of ourselves to Christ, with whom we walk through Lent and through this dappled life.

Day 1

Ash Wednesday

Pied Beauty

Glory be to God for dappled things —
  For skies of couple-colour as a brinded cow;
     For rose-moles all in stipple upon trout that swim;
Fresh-firecoal chestnut-falls; finches' wings;
  Landscape plotted and pieced — fold, fallow, and plough;
     And áll trádes, their gear and tackle and trim.

All things counter, original, spare, strange;
  Whatever is fickle, freckled (who knows how?)
     With swift, slow; sweet, sour; adazzle, dim;
He fathers-forth whose beauty is past change:
                   Praise him.

Our Lenten journey begins in the vividness of God's dappled world. Rich and variegated, shimmering with light and shade, strange, diverse and beautiful, the world of 'Pied Beauty' draws us into the bright and loving creativity of God, through the richness of a uniquely creative poetic vision.

  Over this season, we shall meet Gerard Manley Hopkins in his many shades and moods: through his characteristic flourishes of creative invention; through meaning pouring from the most economic, dextrous and supple of phrases; and through glimpses of a world within our world – a world beyond our world. We will also encounter the poet in expressions of inner torment, spiritual yearning, courage and surrender, through all the seasons and colours of life; and with him, experience dappled human existence. We begin with one of Hopkins' most celebrated poems about God's rich, diverse, dappled world.

'Pied Beauty' – written in perhaps the most poetically exuberant year of Hopkins' life (1877) and during his joyful final years at St Beuno's College in North Wales – begins and ends with praise, embodying Hopkins' belief that our purpose for being is to 'name and praise' God.[4] Between the alpha and omega of praise, we find in 'Pied Beauty' the glorious unfolding of God's presence in the beauty of the world in language so transporting, a style so distinct as to enable a spark not only to leap between *what* we see and us, the seers; it also jumps between the God-given uniqueness of a thing (its 'inscape') and how we experience this – how we 'instress' – the heart and essence of something before us.

We will discover more about Hopkins' 'instress' and 'inscape' as Lent unfolds.[5] For now, it is enough to linger over Hopkins' sense that God gifts to all things their own unique identity or inscape; and that we may experience that inscape through our 'instressing', apprehending and taking in the inscape of another. For Gerard Manley Hopkins, poetry could be a means for this instress: for this transporting experience of touching and being touched by the unique God-given, Christ-given inscape of another.

The first part of this short or 'curtal' sonnet,[6] 'Pied Beauty', pours out before us the piebald beauty of sky, fish, birds: all made more striking by their counterpointing motley.

> Glory be to God for dappled things —
>   For skies of couple-colour as a brinded cow;
>   For rose-moles all in stipple upon trout that swim;
>   Fresh-firecoal chestnut-falls; finches' wings;
>   Landscape plotted and pieced — fold, fallow, and plough;
>   And áll trádes, their gear and tackle and trim.

Objects and creatures have the quality of shot silk, as if shining differently as the light catches them. They are made more striking through analogies with things that are already part of God's dappled world: skies of 'couple-colour' are linked with a 'brinded cow'. And so these two, one of heaven and one of earth, touch and reflect each other in their shared parti-colour, in their flecks and patches of cloud and coat. Even the *sounds* of these opening lines, with their repeated Ps and Bs and hard Cs, create a stippling sound that echoes the 'rose-moles all in stipple upon trout that swim': those distinctive light-shot, pink-banded marks on rainbow trout in their natural habitat.

To earth and sky, Hopkins has added water – and now fire: horse chestnuts become part of this motley world, breaking open as they ripen to reveal their fiery freshness with the intensity of glowing 'firecoal' in a hearth. All of this unfolds in a 'plotted and pieced' patchwork landscape, perhaps reflecting God's design and perhaps simply sharing the variegated human history of an ancient land, patterned with fields held together in echoing and alliterative sounds: 'plotted and pieced – fold, fallow and plough'.

As the poem reaches towards the end of the sonnet's first part, the pace quietens. The poem slows from a quicksilver list to long-stressed sounds and repeated 'ands', which cause us to slow down and to linger. And as we hear about 'áll trádes, their gear and tackle and trim', we are made aware that we are also part of God's dappled world in the immense variety of our lives' crafting.

Then, at the poem's break (the volta), the tone changes. Description gives way to a reflection on the breadth of God's world – but we have to wait for four lines to discover the poet's meaning:

> All things counter, original, spare, strange;
>   Whatever is fickle, freckled (who knows how?)
>   With swift, slow; sweet, sour; adazzle, dim;
> He fathers-forth whose beauty is past change:
>   Praise him.

DAY 1: ASH WEDNESDAY

God 'fathers-forth', says the poet: he gives life to 'all things counter, original, spare, strange', exulting in the sheer variety and difference of all things. More than this, God's presence and beauty are to be found in life's imperfections, in 'whatever is fickle' or 'freckled', too. 'Who knows how?' ponders Hopkins as an aside, as if to hint at the mystery that God, who creates a world of rich and generous difference, should also be discovered at the very heart of what we call imperfection. God 'fathers-forth', says the poet, the 'swift' and 'slow', 'sweet' and 'sour', 'adazzle' and 'dim'. And there is no judgement of one over the other: simply a breathless wonder that all should be birthed within the love of God.

It seems that there is only one response to such creative generosity, and that is to 'Praise him'. Placed at the centre of the final line, this feels final. But praise for Hopkins is what we are here for; and praise, the omega of 'Pied Beauty', is not an ending, but goes on. As we travel through Lent with Hopkins, we will hear time and again his exuberant, faithful celebration of God-with-us. We will discover, too, the shades and the shadows of his life of faith and, as we discover the riches of dappled, faithful humanity caught up in the love of God, we may find ourselves giving glory to God for dappled things.

Praise Him.

Day 2

Thursday

Inversnaid

This darksome burn, horseback brown,
His rollrock highroad roaring down,
In coop and in comb the fleece of his foam
Flutes and low to the lake falls home.

A windpuff-bonnet of fáwn-fróth
Turns and twindles over the broth
Of a pool so pitchblack, féll-fró́wning,
It rounds and rounds Despair to drowning.

Degged with dew, dappled with dew
Are the groins of the braes that the brook treads through,
Wiry heathpacks, flitches of fern,
And the beadbonny ash that sits over the burn.

What would the world be, once bereft
Of wet and of wildness? Let them be left,
O let them be left, wildness and wet;
Long live the weeds and the wilderness yet.

'Long live the weeds and the wilderness yet.'
    On the north-eastern side of Loch Lomond lies the small community of Inversnaid: a place of wild history, outlaws, armies and travellers. Photographs from the 1870s of its toppling waterfalls capture a sepia-tinted wildness that echoes the notes of Hopkins' poem of the same name.

DAY 2: THURSDAY

Written in 1881 on a trip out of Glasgow, 'Inversnaid' emerged in an in-between time in Hopkins' life and work. His peripatetic ministry had taken him, in a few short years, from Sheffield to London, from Oxford to Manchester to Liverpool, and in 1881, briefly to Glasgow. Behind him were the fluid, rich sonnets of God's presence written during his years at St Beuno's and, ahead of him, dappled poems of faith and pain and resurrection. But here, in 'Inversnaid', is a poem of wildness and life-giving wilderness. It celebrates, yearns and laments all at once, describing a life-giving, peace-giving landscape where his muse flared again. Little surprise, then, that this poem dances with life as it takes us downstream through the 'weeds and the wilderness', drawing us into the stream's journey and the light-and-shade transformative nature of wilderness in a landscape filled with God's presence.

From the first verse, we are carried by an insistent rolling rhythm into the '*dark*some burn', opening out to us the inscape of 'Inversnaid', shaped and scoured by this '*horse*back brown' stream as it tumbles on its rocky way. With an energy reminiscent of medieval alliterative verse (like that of *Sir Gawain and the Green Knight*), there is a speed and vigour here intensified by rolling Rs and collapsed descriptions – 'rollrock high road, roaring down' – that hurl us onwards, the stream spilling into every nook and cranny on its way, in 'coop and comb'. Or perhaps on 'his' way, as the 'fleece of *his* foam' brings before us even more deeply the character of this place: the character of a life-force pouring through landscape, with churning spray ('the fleece of his foam'), scouring and singing its way down the hillside.

And then the sounds change. The tumbling river falls 'low' to its lake home; and the roaring and fluting of the first verse gives way to the whisper of churning spray, which 'turns and twindles' over the pool in a 'windpuff-bonnet of fáwn-fróth'.

A windpuff-bonnet of fáwn-fróth
Turns and twindles over the broth
Of a pool so pitchblack, féll-fnówning,
It rounds and rounds Despair to drowning.

INVERSNAID

This second verse seems to form a pivot in the poem: we have tumbled down rocks at speed and find ourselves in the river's 'home' of froth and the 'pitchblack' swirling, bubbling pool. And then we come across a line that may cause us to linger. This churning pool 'rounds and rounds Despair to drowning'.

This is a curious line, introducing 'Despair' as if it were as much a character as the river itself. Perhaps this is an echo of the poet's personal darkness. Or perhaps this place of wildness and wilderness, where Hopkins' muse has flared into life, is a place in which Despair itself may be drowned as it 'rounds and rounds', sucked into the eddying water.

From this pivotal verse, we are drawn into a gentler picture, as if after a storm. The roaring burn (now brae), the swirling pool and deeper hues have given way to a lush landscape, seemingly irrigated by the force that has rushed through it. Everything the river has touched, everything that might have broken its flow – fern, heath or ash – is made 'beadbonny' by sparkling droplets and 'degged [watered] with dew, dappled with dew' in the deep damp of morning freshness. If glory is to be given to God for dappled things, this is a place of God's glory.

After three verses of travelling through the wildness of Inversnaid, from 'darksome burn' to 'beadbonny' brightness, we find ourselves drawn into a plea and a prayer: a plea to those who might replace God's wilderness for one of our designing; and a prayer for the wild places to last:

> What would the world be, once bereft
> Of wet and of wildness? Let them be left,
> O let them be left, wildness and wet;
> Long live the weeds and the wilderness yet.

This plea-prayer, which weaves together humanity's well-being with exuberance and wildness in nature, is spoken in alliterative, inverted, echoing language that brings before us the power and the paradox of wilderness. For Hopkins, this brooding wildness is to be celebrated, loved, kept as a place

DAY 2: THURSDAY

of life-giving beauty, sustaining those who enter it and who 'instress' its essence through a profound encounter. This is the wilderness as a place of journeying and life-giving discovery, with echoes of the paradox of Lenten wilderness, and the discovery that this strange and daunting landscape may become a place of richness, transformation, revelation and new life.

Day 3

Friday

Peace

When will you ever, Peace, wild wooddove, shy wings shut,
Your round me roaming end, and under be my boughs?
When, when, Peacè, will you, Peace? I'll not play hypocrite

To own my heart: I yield you do come sometimes; but
That piecemeal peace is poor peace. What pure peace allows
Alarms of wars, the daunting wars, the death of it?

O surely, reaving Peace, my Lord should leave in lieu
Some good! And so he does leave Patience exquisite,
That plumes to Peace thereafter. And when Peace here
   does house
He comes with work to do, he does not come to coo,
         He comes to brood and sit.

In July 1883, Gerard Manley Hopkins wrote to his friend Robert Bridges from Stonyhurst College, Lancashire: 'It is likely that I shall be removed; where I have no notion. But I have long been Fortune's football ...'[7]

In the preceding years, Hopkins' vocation had called him on every few months. From St Beuno's, which had nourished his muse, he went in 1877 to teach in Sheffield, before moving (with the briefest of notices) to Stonyhurst College and then to Farm Street Church in Mayfair. A transfer to St Aloysius' Church in Oxford followed, before he was called on to Lancashire and then Liverpool: all by the end of 1879. Perhaps it is no surprise, with such instability, that when another move beckoned late in that year, he wrote the compact and powerfully moving poem 'Peace'.

Like his better-known 'Pied Beauty', 'Peace' is a 'curtal sonnet'. In its form, it shows us something of Hopkins' sheer poetic creativity. Shorter than the traditional sonnet but built on the same proportions (with 10 and a half lines rather than 14), these curtal sonnets seem to move with a different intensity from their longer poetic siblings, not least because Hopkins was trying to 'do in 10 and a half lines what other sonnets were doing in 14'.[8] 'Peace', for example, a plea, a meditation on the nature of and our desire for peace, appears both languorous and meaning-full for all its shorter form. Here, we find Hopkins' shifting voice and lilting, echoing language occupying a denser space, and leaving us with a half line that seems both to complete the whole and to open a space beyond the poem. All this is evoked in ten and a half lines of exploratory, reverberating and alliterative verse that moves quickly in its moods and turns.

To begin with, Hopkins speaks directly to Peace, partly pleading for peace to come, partly acknowledging its presence, while lamenting that it is neither as fulsome nor as all-embracing as he wants it to be. The poem weaves yearningly through waves of sound that curl back on themselves as if to create a sense of peace's longed-for, absent warm embrace:

> When will you ever, Peace, wild wooddove, shy wings shut,
> Your round me roaming end, and under be my boughs?
> When, when, Peacè, will you, Peace?

Peace, we hear, is a 'wild wooddove', with 'shy wings shut', conjuring a familiar wistful birdsong, amplified by the gentle fricative of 'shy wings shut'. But this 'wild wooddove' Peace is moving, 'roaming' rather than settling and nestling with the poet. Peace circles Hopkins but doesn't land with him, which leads to the pleading question, 'When, when, Peacè, will you, Peace?' as if echoing the wooddove's characteristic song ('when, when'). 'Peace', as the one addressed, now seems to blend into a verb, as if peace will not be itself for him: peace will not 'peace'.

As the poems shifts and moves into the second of the group of four lines, the focus and direction of the poem begin to change. Still addressing Peace, the poet says in slightly startling terms, 'I'll not play hypocrite / To own my heart': he does sometimes know peace; but the peace he knows is partial, lean and always limited by the vagaries of life and by its own imminent flight from him:

>   I'll not play hypocrite
> To own my heart: I yield you do come sometimes; but
> That piecemeal peace is poor peace. What pure peace allows
> Alarms of wars, the daunting wars, the death of it?

As if to underline that peace can be scattered and finite, the metre slightly changes. Though written in a formal pattern of syllables and stresses,[9] in which each line comprises two groups of six syllables, 'Peace' shifts to a more piecemeal pattern to express that 'piecemeal peace is poor peace'. Two stressed words chasing each other ('poor peace'), their stress echoed in 'pure peace' in the same line, shift us towards a searching question. What kind of 'pure' peace is it, the poet asks, that permits the threat of wars to hover and so bring about its own 'death'?

Now, the poem goes through its greatest shift in thought and mood. In the final lines, Hopkins turns to reflect on the nature of peace and God; and he guides himself (and us) towards a new vision of peace, which is more than the absence of war:

> O surely, reaving Peace, my Lord should leave in lieu
> Some good! And so he does leave Patience exquisite,
> That plumes to Peace thereafter. And when Peace here
>   does house
> He comes with work to do, he does not come to coo,
>   He comes to brood and sit.

DAY 3: FRIDAY

If we are robbed of peace, muses Hopkins, surely God leaves something else – 'some good' – in its place. The answer is that, yes, God does. And the 'good' we are offered is 'Patience': the patience in which we wait for the peace we desire. 'Exquisite' patience, we hear, seems to shake out its feathers and 'plume' to Peace, returning to us the wooddove of the opening line, no longer with 'shy wings shut'. Now, when Peace does arrive through Patience, it comes 'with work to do': it has 'not come to coo' but to 'brood and sit'. This is peace transformed, no longer quiet with nestling wings; no longer imagined as an absence of distress; and not piecemeal. This is peace as an active presence, come to do the 'work' of bringing something to birth within us – to 'brood and sit' as we are shaped by the love of God.

This Lent, we may be seeking peace in the midst of overfilled lives, in the midst of uncertainty or fracture. Hopkins' 'Peace' may leave us with the understanding that our cry for peace is valid. So, too, may it leave us feeling called to re-understand the peace we crave; to allow the peace that is birthed in patience to transform us as, when Peace does come,

> He comes with work to do, he does not come to coo,
>   He comes to brood and sit.

Day 4

Saturday

Moonrise June 19 1876

I awoke in the Midsummer not-to-call night, | in the white
and the walk of the morning:
The moon, dwindled and thinned to the fringe | of a
finger-nail held to the candle,
Or paring of paradisaïcal fruit, | lovely in waning but
lustreless,
Stepped from the stool, drew back from the barrow, | of
dark Maenefa the mountain;
A cusp still clasped him, a fluke yet fanged him, | entangled
him, not quit utterly.
This was the prized, the desirable sight, | unsought,
presented so easily,
Parted me leaf and leaf, divided me, | eyelid and eyelid
of slumber.

Just to the east of St Beuno's, Hopkins' home for three years from 1874 to 1877, rises Moel Maenefa, the Rock of Eve. Though far from being one of Wales's highest, this is a hill that dominates the surrounding area.

With the Dee estuary to the east and the Vale of Clwyd to the west, Maenefa occupies a between-place in an ancient landscape, in the thinnest part of the Clwydian hills in north-east Wales. These are hills that take us back to the distant Silurian age of colliding continents, as the land that is now Wales moved, and still moves, 'at about the same rate our fingernails grow';[10] a seemingly eternal place but always shifting with a barely discernible progression, like the travelling moon.

DAY 4: SATURDAY

This between place, both still and moving, was brought to life by Hopkins in 'Moonrise June 19 1876'. Though not among his most well-known verse, this midsummer-poem gives us a glimpse of a seemingly still point in summer as the waning moon hovers over eternal hills. To linger over 'Moonrise' is to discover a mesmerizing moment, shimmering in pellucid light, in a poem playing with a tantalizing form, unusual stresses and a still moment hanging in time gifted to the poet and shared with us. This is an everywhere, all-time moment (but securely located in Wales on 19 June 1876), as the waning moon, fading in brightness in the stop-go of time, hung over Maenefa. So arresting, so particular was this moment for Hopkins that the force of its inscape seemed to reach and meet him in a moment of profound instress.

'Moonrise' offers us something different in the body of Hopkins' work. When it originally appeared in Robert Bridges' edition of Hopkins' poetry in 1918, it was in the section 'unfinished poems and fragments'; but whether it was unfinished is uncertain. With its seven lines, each with seven stresses and each with a mid-line break between the fourth and fifth stresses, there seems to be a certain completeness to 'Moonrise'. Each crafted line ends with a word that falls aways unstressed, creating a sound-pattern that leaves us floating in the dappled moonrise, with a trailing, languid quality: '*mor*ning', we hear, '*can*dle', '*lustre*less', '*moun*tain', '*utter*ly', '*easi*ly', '*slum*ber'. This is not a sonnet; and yet to break each line fully at Hopkins' mid-line break would be to create a kind of curious sonnet – unrhymed and with uneven stresses – but comprising 14 lines, with a shift in tone between the first eight lines and the last six. It is not a sonnet but it has the structural echoes of a sonnet, exploring the play between three characters: the poet, the moon and Maenefa.

The poem begins and ends with the poet framing his response to the moon, which seems to call him out of sleep and fill him with wonder:

MOONRISE JUNE 19 1876

> I awoke in the Midsummer not-to-call night, | in the white
>   and the walk of the morning:
> The moon, dwindled and thinned to the fringe | of a
>   finger-nail held to the candle,
> Or paring of paradisaïcal fruit, | lovely in waning but
>   lustreless,
> Stepped from the stool, drew back from the barrow, | of
>   dark Maenefa the mountain;

We seem to see with Hopkins, as he wakes in the not-fully-dark summer night, the silver light of the moon as it 'walks' towards the morning, echoing Hopkins' own habit of walking the hills around St Beuno's at the break of day. This is a moon that is 'lovely in waning but lustreless'; a moon in that phase when shadows are cast which reveal its imperfect, dappled surface. And when it is slimmed to the slenderest of glowing arcs, it is, says Hopkins, as if we held a fingernail in front of a candle and saw the faintest glimmer of light shine through its milky tip; or as if it were the finest sliver of an apple, a 'paring of paradisaïcal fruit' – slight, pale and translucent – this is a moonrise that carries the seed of its own waning, like the fruit of paradise it resembles.

And then the moon, seeming so diaphanous in its progress through the summer sky, comes more sharply into view. It seems suspended in time in this ancient place, with its ancient burial mound ('barrow'), and somehow acts upon both Maenefa and the poet:

> A cusp still clasped him, a fluke yet fanged him, | entangled
>   him, not quit utterly.
> This was the prized, the desirable sight, | unsought,
>   presented so easily,
> Parted me leaf and leaf, divided me, | eyelid and eyelid
>   of slumber.

The musical alliteration of ancient dialect words seems to fix us even more sharply in time and place to a still moment, as

DAY 4: SATURDAY

the mountain seems to be held fast – 'clasped' by the 'cusp' of the moon – by those sharp points where translucent arc and shadowed moon meet. It is 'fanged' (seized hold of and held tight, as if prey) by the moon's 'fluke', with all the associations of the barb of an arrow or tips of a whale's tail in all its overwhelming immensity. And it holds Hopkins, too, in a moment of apparent epiphany as this 'prized', 'desirable sight' rises to meet him 'unsought, presented so easily'. This is a graced moment, offering us a glimpse of our desiring search met in the Giver of all gifts, who presents us 'so easily' with so graced a vision. It is also a threshold moment in and out of time; a moment of stillness and movement, ancient and immediate at a summer's turn, with its own unique character and essence – its own inscape. In the final breathtaking line of 'Moonrise', we are offered a glimpse of Hopkins' profound instress of this moment. He is filled with a vision that enters his soul with a gentle sharpness and an overwhelming sense of being met, in the most fine-grained, most textured of ways: he is 'parted ... leaf and leaf', like the finest of tissue-pages being separated and read. In the blink of sleeping and waking, 'eyelid and eyelid of slumber', the diaphanous, immense moon greets him.

'Moonrise' leaves us with a glimpse of grace and awakening rooted in a moment in time. We may also be left with the hint of a greater awakening to the grace and life of the one who travels with us ('*un*sought, *pre*sented *so* easily'), enters our hearts ('*leaf* and *leaf*') and draws us ('*ey*elid and *ey*elid of *slum*ber') to awaken to his life, moment by moment and in eternity.

Day 5

Monday

Hope Holds to Christ

Hope holds to Christ the mind's own mirror out
To take His lovely likeness more and more.
It will not well, so she would bring about
A growing burnish brighter than before
And turns to wash it from her welling eyes
And breaths the blots of all with sighs and sighs.

Her glass is blest but she as good as blind
Holds till hand aches and wonders what is there;
Her glass drinks light, she darkles down behind,
All of her glorious gainings unaware.
I told you that she turned her mirror dim
Betweenwhiles, but she sees herself not him.

Imagine for a moment a gossamer-fine spider's web, brightening the dark of a frosty winter dawn or carrying the dew of a freshly irrigated world. Its fragile thread is easily lost in life's vagaries; yet woven into life-sustaining, gravity defying canopies of light, it is strong enough to bear up all who rely on its high-wire world.

We may know hope as a gossamer presence, at once sustaining and fleeting, brightly iridescent but easily pulled apart by searching hearts. In one moment, a glorious presence and in another a flickering absence, hope can seem to arrive and depart, according to dappled hearts and circumstance; and if it becomes more fragile than sustaining, it can leave us untethered from life and faith. Hope like this, fragile and fickle, may be the hope that *we* have; but there is a greater hope that has *us*, woven into the life-sustaining, load-bearing fabric of the world, undergirding our lives. *This* is hope that is ours and not ours, that we may have and lose, but that always has – and does not lose – *us*.

To be true to the experience of hope, in its gossamer fragility and undergirding strength, is not only to call upon the very human emotional textures of hope as it ebbs and flows; it is also to dwell in the deeper contours of the hope that lies at the heart of our journey of life and faith, encompassing and sustaining us. More than any 'transfiguring glow superimposed upon a darkened existence',[11] as Jürgen Moltmann put it, this is hope that is utterly rooted in the present and the eternal as it courses through dappled lives; it is also rooted in a reality that 'knows and sees and holds who we are and have been'.[12]

Here, we draw close to the complexity of hope that Hopkins explores in 'Hope Holds to Christ'. As creatures of faith, we may know not only the firm ground of a hope that knows, sees and holds us, but also the challenge of gossamer-fine hope that seems to spill and slide through fingers reaching out for its promise of life. Hopkins' gift in this poem is to evoke both of these: to hold together the complexity of the hope that we have and the hope that has us; and to explore how hope lives in the human heart and mind. Here, hope is almost a 'third' (personified as female) who is both a gift of God in Christ and also embedded in humanity: recipient and bearer of that gift which we yearn for but may struggle to accept or nurture.

The opening two lines of the poem immediately offer us more texture than the title suggests. No sooner have we heard that personified Hope '*holds to* Christ' – as if 'holding fast' to Christ for her own existence and meaning – than the word 'out' appears. This takes us to a relationship between Hope and Christ that is somehow more gentle, distant and yet absorbing: hope holds *out* the mirror of the human mind to Christ so that his image might be captured and reflected within the mind of the beholder:

> Hope holds to Christ the mind's own mirror out
> To take His lovely likeness more and more.

There is a simple clarity to these lines; but we are invited to savour their depth as sound and tempo shift through alliteration and repetition. There is an aspirant speed to 'Hope Holds to Christ' that shifts to a slower register in the strongly stressed, more nasal and elongated 'mind's own mirror' before we are allowed to hear the meaning-shifting word 'out', which draws us into the second line. Alliteration ('To take', 'lovely likeness') carries us on again towards the repeated sounds of 'more and more', as if the likeness of Christ is thirstily drunk. In these two short lines, personified Hope has a timeless, almost angelic quality, as if an intermediary rooted in both the human and the divine, holding together the gift of Christ and our human capacity to receive and absorb that gift.

Yet, we hear that 'it will not well'. It seems that we struggle to absorb Christ's 'lovely likeness' through the mind's mirror, so Hope tries harder to polish the mirror – to 'bring about / A growing burnish brighter than before'. We are not told the source of this struggle, whether it is due to the vagaries of ordinary living, the human heart or simply that human hope is only hope when our limitations, sadness and despair call her into necessary life. Perhaps it is all these things; so the 'mind's own mirror' is most brightly burnished when heartbreak and hope meet, and she

> ... turns to wash it from her welling eyes
> And breaths the blots of all with sighs and sighs.

In an echo of the 'will not well' of earlier, Hope washes the mind's mirror with tears from her 'welling eyes'. The breath of her sighs allows the mirror's obscuring blots to be cleared, as when we breathe on glass and shine the vapoured dimness away, becoming again a kind of mediator in the dance of humanity and divine gift. And then we are invited to find out more about hope in an image that seems to conflate the mind's mirror and her own:

DAY 5: MONDAY

> Her glass is blest but she as good as blind
> Holds till hand aches and wonders what is there;
> Her glass drinks light, she darkles down behind,
> All of her glorious gainings unaware.

As the bearer of a 'blest' mirror, Hope tries to absorb and reflect the glory of Christ but she is tucked behind this glass (which we might imagine as a mirror pointing away from her) and is unable to grasp the glory she reflects. There may be a distant echo here, almost a reverse echo of Romans 8.24, in which we hear that 'hope that is seen is not hope. For who hopes for what is seen?' Here, it seems to be Hope herself who does not see; and yet she continues to hold the mirror until she is weary with holding, 'till hand aches' and she 'wonders what is there'. This Hope is persistent, beyond tiredness, beyond incomprehension, in her desire to absorb the 'lovely likeness' of Christ; her *'glass drinks'*, we hear (in a double, dogged stress), as she '*dark*les *down* be*hind*', hinting at Hope's shadow-cast shivering even as she tries to reflect Christ's glory. There is something poignant, too, about these workings of Hope, who reaches – both deeply into the emotional, faithful texture of our dappled lives and outwards towards the one who gives us all that is beyond our capacity to generate or contain – to carry us through life's vagaries. Yet, Hope here is unaware of 'all her glorious gainings', even while burnishing the mind to receive more deeply Christ's 'lovely likeness'. This is no 'transfiguring glow superimposed upon a darkened existence';[13] it is a hope that reaches beyond itself and is rooted in a reality that 'knows and sees and holds who we are and have been'.[14]

The last two lines of 'Hope Holds to Christ' seem to have a different character. In these lines, which are sometimes printed as a separate couplet, it is as if the poet turns to address us and we are invited in to reflect on them, asking questions of Hope and of ourselves. 'I told you', says the poet, 'that she turned her mirror dim / Betweenwhiles.' There may be a hint here that when human Hope loses the ability or will to reach beyond herself, she grows dim and turns inwards; and the poet's turn towards us may act as a kind of echo-chamber, emphasizing Hope's change of focus. Or perhaps we are left with the suggestion that our vision of Hope and Christ will always be dimmed in this 'betweenwhiles' state of earthly life, in which we 'see in a mirror, dimly' until we can see 'face to face'.[15]

> I told you that she turned her mirror dim
> Betweenwhiles, but she sees herself not him.

However we read these final lines, we may be left with a sense of the gift of humanly felt, divinely rooted Hope that fires hearts and souls, which may turn inwards but are equally capable of hopeful faith. This is the hope we may know in our lives: it is richest when turning its face towards Christ and burnishing the mind's mirror to become the Hope of Christ in and beyond our earthly life.

In Lent, as we walk with Christ, we may come to know this hope more fully as we explore the hope we carry and the hope that carries us, catching us up in the Hope beyond our hope: in the hope of God in Christ. Gossamer Hope, finely spun and brightening the dark of frosted lives, irrigating the mind's mirror; delicate and steel-strong thread, easily drawn apart and dimmed; and yet woven into life-sustaining, gravity-defying canopies of light by the one who holds our world in his gentle strength.

> Hope holds to Christ the mind's own mirror out
> To take His lovely likeness more and more.

Day 6

Tuesday

Carrion Comfort

Not, I'll not, carrion comfort, Despair, not feast on thee;
Not untwist — slack they may be — these last strands of man
In me ór, most weary, cry I can no more. I can;
Can something, hope, wish day come, not choose not to be.
But ah, but O thou terrible, why wouldst thou rude on me
Thy wring-world right foot rock? lay a lionlimb against
   me? scan
With darksome devouring eyes my bruisèd bones? and fan,
O in turns of tempest, me heaped there; me frantic to avoid
   thee and flee?

Why? That my chaff might fly; my grain lie, sheer and clear.
Nay in all that toil, that coil, since (seems) I kissed the rod,
Hand rather, my heart lo! lapped strength, stole joy, would
   laugh, chéer.

Cheer whom though? the hero whose heaven-handling
   flung me, fóot tród
Me? or me that fought him? O which one? is it each one?
   That night, that year
Of now done darkness I wretch lay wrestling with
   (my God!) my God.

The journey of Lent towards the Passion can take us through some of the most authentic experiences and expressions of faith. Questioning, restlessness, glimpses of God's glory and hope-filled yearning all have a place on this path, as we accompany Christ through the wilderness and beyond. Our steps on the path may be bold or stumbling. We may find ourselves drawn along in the slipstream of God's glory, or falteringly offering our questions, our doubts and fears to the one who knows all, receives all, forgives all.

Hopkins' 'Terrible Sonnets' (or 'Sonnets of Desolation') can be a guide along this path of questioning and discovery. Written in the mid 1880s during his final, troubled years in Dublin,[16] these sonnets offer so powerful a blend of faith and struggle that, as with the psalms, we may discover echoes of our own questions, doubts and hopes. 'Carrion Comfort' is just such a poem. With its ambivalence and authenticity, it seems to ask what it means to be true both to the struggles of life and the demands of faith when we are caught between a desire for new life and comfortable, desolate inertia.

There is a terrible beauty to this poem of faithful wrestling, written at a time of personal struggle for Hopkins. Around this time, he wrote to his friend Robert Bridges: 'In the life I lead now, which is one of a continually jaded and harassed mind, if in any leisure, I try to do anything, I make no way – nor with my work, alas! But so it must be.'[17]

In the same letter he wrote: 'I do not despair, things might change ... only there is no great appearance of it.' We hear the echoes of this dejected stasis and nearly-hope in 'Carrion Comfort', which is shot through with the struggle to be a disciple of a God who doesn't play by the rules of easy glory. From the very beginning, the poet seems to be looking for a language to do justice to experience, faith and feeling. Words move restlessly but somehow emphatically, amplified through repetition so that meaning doubles back on itself. There is rhyming within lines, meaning lying across lines and an uncertain, shifting focus for Hopkins' poetic cry. He invites us into his shifting world of prayerful, faithful, anguished struggle, in search of a meaning in the mystery of God's ways to humanity. In a series of negatives, the poet begins:

DAY 6: TUESDAY

> Not, I'll not, carrion comfort, Despair, not feast on thee;
> Not untwist — slack they may be — these last strands of man
> In me ór, most weary, cry I can no more. I can;
> Can something, hope, wish day come, not choose not to be.

These negatives seem like an attempt by Hopkins to convince someone (perhaps himself, perhaps God or a personified Despair) of the emotional, faith-challenged and faith-challenging argument that he weaves. '*Not*, I'll *not*,' he begins, as if banging the table with his fist, '*not* feast on thee; / *Not* untwist ... these last strands of man / In me.' He refuses to feed on 'carrion comfort, Despair' and become unravelled. Emphatic as this is though, the repetitions seem to loop back and hint, too, at the opposite: 'I'll not ... not feast on thee.' So from the beginning, Hopkins' words and sounds dance together to paint a whole landscape of human experience; the spectre of 'carrion comfort, Despair' looms and is fought but still hovers.

But whether Hopkins is addressing 'Despair' or 'carrion comfort' is uncertain. We might hear in these words: 'I won't despair, carrion comfort, I won't feast on you.' Or our thoughts might slide to 'I won't feast on you, despair, you are carrion comfort'. We might hear a battle with the deathly ('carrion') comfort to stop from sinking into despair; or we might hear the seductive lure of the grave for one in despair. Or we might hear the seduction of an earthly life not quickened by faith, a 'carrion' life, comfortable in its rejection of the life and challenge of Christ with us: the lure and a trap of a death in life.

As the poem tumbles on, we seem to slip into the worst of fears and then rise again, in the line-breaking refusal to unravel, to 'untwist – slack they may be – these last strands of man / In me.' The poet seems beyond tears ('cry I can no more') but then the mood shifts and turns; in a flurry of rapid sounds, we hear intimations of hope:

> I can;
> Can something, hope, wish day come, not choose not to be.

He *can* '*not* choose not to be': he can choose to live. But still the questions go on, now seemingly addressed towards God and, in a flurry of allusions, to suffering. 'Thou terrible,' we hear, 'why wouldst thou rude on me?' 'Why make me suffer? Why treat me with such violence?' he seems to ask, with a sound-echo of the suffering of the cross ('rude'/rood). The rolling repetitive R in 'wring-world right' seems to draw out the agony further, conjuring for us the force of God who, with leonine power,[18] lays 'a lionlimb' against him and turns 'darksome devouring eyes' upon him, so that the one lamenting wants to 'turn and flee'.

'Why wouldst thou rude on me ...?' he has asked. This 'why' now finds an echo and partial response in the sestet, as Hopkins takes us through a twisting, turning argument through why he might be suffering. 'Why?' he asks again:

Why? That my chaff might fly; my grain lie, sheer and clear.

In emphatic, echoing, rhyming language, we hear that he is called to discover what it means to be refined and to be left with intimations of new life. In the 'sheer and clear' of the grain left when chaff has flown, the potential for this new life may be laid bare: through suffering we barely understand; we may discover both our losses and our possibilities. We may even 'laugh' and 'cheer' in our intensity of experience. 'Cheer whom though?' asks Hopkins, shifting again:

Cheer whom though? the hero whose heaven-handling
    flung me, fóot tród
Me? or me that fought him? O which one? is it each one?
    That night, that year
Of now done darkness I wretch lay wrestling with
    (my God!) my God.

Is he to cheer the God whose ways seem a kind of heroic bravado: this 'heaven-handling' God who 'flings' and tramples his creatures? Or is the poet to cheer himself for the fight he has put up? Or both ('is it each one?'). As 'Carrion Comfort' draws to a close, it seems that the endless ('that night, that year') agonies are passing. The 'darkness' is 'now done' and, in the cry of one who has been 'wrestling with (my God!) my God', we discern the echo of the Cross.[19] We may hear in these words the deepest and most profound cry of humanity; we may hear the pain, rage and pity of Christ, wrestling with the 'heaven-handling' that has flung him among us, called to know the depths of our own agonies. Yet these are also words we cannot read without knowing that they point beyond themselves, through a darkness that, though ink-black, will give way to light.

In this poem of twists and turns and doubling back, we may finally find ourselves looping back to the start of 'Carrion Comfort'. The struggle of the Cross and the merest glimpse of light that *might* hint at resurrection, may draw us back to the strangely restless, strangely emphatic words of the poem's beginning: 'Not, I'll not, carrion comfort, Despair, not feast on thee.' In this, we may find echoes of our own twisting, turning stories of faith in which we step forward and double back; look ahead, then avert our eyes. But gradually, gradually, we draw close to Christ who draws us on towards intimations of hope, which the carrion comfort of the grave could not and cannot hold.

Day 7

Wednesday

Heaven-Haven

A nun takes the veil

   I have desired to go
      Where springs not fail,
To fields where flies no sharp and sided hail
   And a few lilies blow.

   And I have asked to be
      Where no storms come,
Where the green swell is in the havens dumb,
   And out of the swing of the sea.

There is a sweetness, serenity and simplicity about this brief, early poem of Gerard Manley Hopkins. Written while he was an undergraduate in Oxford, it does not yet have the flourishes of the mature poet or the creative complexity of language and syntax; but there is still a distinctive texture to 'Heaven-Haven'. It is the sort of texture that comes with entering a liminal space, lingering on a threshold and looking ahead, caught for a moment in the possibility that draws us on and yearning for the peace we may find.

Perhaps it is no surprise that a quietly iridescent poem in search of peace and serenity should be written during Hopkins' intense student years of poetry, friendship and spiritual seeking. On a threshold himself, Hopkins had not yet reached his decision to become a Roman Catholic; but it seems that possibilities of the religious life were already beginning to shape him. And here, in 'Heaven-Haven', speaking in the voice of 'a nun tak[ing] the veil', Hopkins draws us into the dreams and hopes of a religious as they contemplate their life ahead, in this world and the next.

The very title 'Heaven-Haven'[20] seems to hover between worlds, as the 'haven' – the sanctuary – of the religious life and the haven of eternal life are both brought before us. As the poem unfolds, this hovering between worlds continues as Hopkins' language somehow plays with time. Both brief verses begin with a nod to time past and time to come. 'I have desired to go', the nun says in the first verse, and 'I have asked to be' in the second; and as we read the poem, it is as if we, too, find ourselves, with this soon-to-be-sister, on the threshold of something new in that waiting space between desire and fulfilment.

The desire, we hear in the second verse, is to go to a place where 'springs not fail', with echoes of the living water flowing 'out of the believer's heart': the believer who goes to Christ in thirst.[21] The desire, too, is to go to a landscape where we are not assailed by the piercing sting of all that life throws at us with the intensity of horizontal ('sided') hail; it is to go to a place where there are 'a few lilies', which move ('blow') in the swaying breeze. Or perhaps this 'blow' is the more ancient 'bloom' or 'blossom', conjuring before us flowering lilies, with their reminders of sacredness and purity in the place of peace.

If the nun taking the veil has 'desired to go / Where springs not fail', so too has she 'asked to be / Where no storms come': to be in a safe-haven, which may be the seclusion of the convent or the promise of eternity. As the verse unfolds, we are taken through the contours of this haven untouched by storms. This is less a place of living waters irrigating the soul than a place of refuge from the overwhelming currents of life. Here, the 'green swell' and churn of the ocean are silenced (made 'dumb') and all is protected from the natural hurl – the 'swing' – of the sea. By the end of the verse, it is as if we have been brought into that haven, which is a place of peace, silence and calm even when the storms rage outside.

HEAVEN-HAVEN

The gentle movement of 'Heaven-Haven', which draws us towards living waters and then calm waters, is expressed in a simplicity of language and gentleness of cadence that mirrors the calm of the haven. We may find that we are also brought into a place of peace as we linger over its gentle movement and breeze-sighing sounds; and yet perhaps the peace may not be quite as simple as it seems.

There is a certain innocence in this poem, perhaps of one (whether nun or poet) who has yet to discover that even a place of apparent peace may not be free of the storms that rise to meet us simply because we are alive. But whether we see this as an innocent poem or not, we might nevertheless recognize the cry of one who seeks God's peace in life's storms as our own cry for peace; our own desire for living waters and for a safe-haven, here and in eternity.

On our Lenten journey, we may discover our own threshold of yearning and possibility. And we may find ourselves surrendering to the one who gifts us living waters and draws us to him through life's passions and storms: to our Heaven-Haven.

Day 8

Thursday

The Lantern Out of Doors

Sometimes a lantern moves along the night,
   That interests our eyes. And who goes there?
   I think; where from and bound, I wonder, where,
With, all down darkness wide, his wading light?

Men go by me whom either beauty bright
   In mould or mind or what not else makes rare:
   They rain against our much-thick and marsh air
Rich beams, till death or distance buys them quite.

Death or distance soon consumes them: wind
   What most I may eye after, be in at the end
I cannot, and out of sight is out of mind.

Christ minds: Christ's interest, what to avow or amend
   There, éyes them, heart wánts, care haúnts, foot Fóllows
     kínd,
Their ránsom, théir rescue, ánd first, fást, last friénd.

In October 1877, it was time for Hopkins to leave St Beuno's, his home for three years. It had been here that his distinct, transporting poetic style had been birthed; it had been here that the God-given uniqueness of things (their *haecceitas*: inscape) had been instressed – woven into new landscapes of meaning – and leapt from his verse.

   Now Hopkins was leaving this place of grace and gift where, in his final months, he had faltered in his exams as he prepared for ministry. Whether the result of his erratic health, perceived theological eccentricities or some other reason,[22] this meant that a fourth year of study was not open to him. Hopkins was called to reconcile himself to a different future from the one he might have expected and a different ministry, and to leaving for places that sang less to his soul.

In the days before his move, and just days after Hopkins' ordination as a priest, St Beuno's left its mark in a final sonnet. 'The Lantern Out of Doors' is a poem of beauty, loss and transience. It somehow captures the mood of this time, when hope seemed to falter as he reflected on constancy and change – and on the place of Christ in his life. The poem opens with a line of exquisite brevity and fleeting beauty in a picture of light that Hopkins was to reverse in his later poem 'The Candle Indoors'. In both poems, his attention is caught by the glow of a light. But while in 'The Candle Indoors' that light is the soft yellow glow of a candle illuminating the interior as the poet walks the dark streets, in 'The Lantern Out of Doors' that light moves outside as the poet watches from within and muses on the light that lives in those who pass by, capturing the attention of the watcher as they travel on their way.

In the first line of 'The Lantern' (as in its later companion poem), the word 'sometimes' appears, both placing and unplacing the action of the poem. 'Sometimes a lantern moves along the night', we hear; suddenly, we seem to find ourselves in a place of our imagining, or in a place of memory or a place of dreams, as the 'sometimes' light catches the eye of the beholder. And the sound echoes of 'where', 'wonder', 'where', 'with', 'wide', 'wading' seem to open out the vision of darkness with the tiniest pinprick of travelling light.

'And who goes there?' the poet asks. Where is this light coming from and what is its destination? Now the lantern's light seems to become the light of those who walk by: those whose 'rich beams' pour out – 'rain' – against seemingly impenetrable darkness until their light is spent by 'death or distance'. This light emerges from beauty; but not only the obviously beautiful. Hopkins sees beauty in 'mould or mind

DAY 8: THURSDAY

or *what not else*'; this is a kind of ordinary beauty of dappled souls who carry a light simply by being and passing by; who rain 'rich beams' against the darkness that would otherwise be impenetrable.

> Men go by me whom either beauty bright
>   In mould or mind or what not else makes rare:
>   They rain against our much-thick and marsh air
> Rich beams, till death or distance buys them quite.

There is light here; and beauty and ordinariness and transience in these lines, perhaps bringing before us the poet's deep care for those whose light flickers in and out of our view: fireflies with us for an instant and then gone. Or perhaps here we find a gentle, haunting lament in which Hopkins prepares his heart for the losses of loved fellow students, who pass out of sight as he prepares to leave St Beuno's.

Then we are drawn into the sestet (the last six lines of the poem), in a curious blend of turn and continuity; the first of these lines echoes the last of the octet (the first eight lines that open the sonnet), with the repetition of 'death or distance':

> They rain against our much-thick and marsh air
> Rich beams, till death or distance buys them quite.
>
> Death or distance soon consumes them: wind
>   What most I may eye after, be in at the end
> I cannot...

We have lingered in the light of the lantern, on the lantern-bearer and on the light we carry; but now, with the haunting repetition of 'death and distance', we are called to follow the poet's gaze, staring after the winding path of the flickering light as it fades and disappears. 'Death or distance soon consumes them,' and the poet recognizes that it is not for him – for any of us – to hold on to the spark of light beyond its time. There is a strange stillness in the emphatic words 'be in at the end / I cannot, and out of sight is out of mind'; and then there is another repetition and another turn.

>   ... be in at the end
>   I cannot, and out of sight is out of mind.
>
>   Christ minds: Christ's interest, what to avow or amend
>   There, éyes them, heart wánts, care haúnts, foot Fóllows
>   kínd,
>   Their ránsom, théir rescue, ánd first, fást, last friend.

We may be lost to one another by death or distance; we may fade from memory as light fades and so become 'out of mind'; but we are never gone from the care of Christ. 'Christ minds,' says the poet. In these last six lines,[23] with their echoing stresses and merging sounds ('wind', 'end', 'mind', 'amend', 'kind', 'friend'), we hear the insistent footfall of following love, with us even to death. This is the Saviour who gazes and yearns, 'haunted' by care for us and following us as we follow him.

This is the one who spent his life for us and who remains our 'first, fást, last friénd', the lantern we eternally carry and cannot help but follow: our 'ransom', our 'rescue' and 'first, fást, last friénd'.

Day 9

Friday

The Candle Indoors

Some candle clear burns somewhere I come by.
I muse at how its being puts blissful back
With yellowy moisture mild night's blear-all black,
Or to-fro tender trambeams truckle at the eye.

By that window what task what fingers ply,
I plod wondering, a-wanting, just for lack
Of answer the eagerer a-wanting Jessy or Jack
There God to aggrándise, God to glorify.—

Come you indoors, come home; your fading fire
Mend first and vital candle in close heart's vault:
You there are master, do your own desire;

What hinders? Are you beam-blind, yet to a fault
In a neighbour deft-handed? Are you that liar
And, cast by conscience out, spendsavour salt?

In June 1879, Hopkins sent two sonnets to his friend Bridges. 'I am afraid they are not very good,' he said. 'One is a companion to the "Lantern", not at first meant to be though, but it fell in.'[24] Written two years after 'The Lantern Out of Doors', this was 'The Candle Indoors': a poem of searing self-reflection and profound gentleness; rooted in the image of a candle's glow. Unlike the travelling lantern of the earlier poem, 'The Candle Indoors' carries us into house, home and heart. Light and dark play together in this intensely moving poem of the inner and the outer, of faith and fear, and desire and doubt, with candlelight picturing the inscape of both a home's flame and a heart's warmth.

In the first part of this sonnet, the octet draws us into accompanying the poet as he walks in the dark of night and catches glimpses of the glow of candlelight, reaching outside from indoors and smudging the dense gloom. There is a soft focus to this opening picture: not only in the yellow light but also in the languor and lilt of the language, and the gently sibilant alliteration of 'some candle' burning 'somewhere'. This repeated 'some' seems to turn a specific moment into many moments, which reach (like candlelight) into dark corners and recesses of mind and memory. Here is a glow that calls us out but which must be tended within.

The candle indoors, says Hopkins, simply in its 'being' causes the 'blear-all black' of the night to recede: the light seems to dilute or dissolve with 'yellowy moisture' the obscuring darkness. This has the feel of an intimate, ancient light, offering a gentle yellow glow at a time when lighting was being transformed by the harsher brightness of gas and electricity; it is a light that seems to speak more of inner illumination than outer clarity. Yet this so-gentle light from indoors is able to make its way to another, in the rich and complex image of 'to-fro tender trambeams' that 'truckle at the eye'.

The sound alone – with its alliterative pull and stressed T syllables, softened by longer, gentler elongated syllables ('*to*-fro'; '*ten*der'; '*tram*beams') – shimmers with the gentle movement of candlelight; perhaps with flickering soft threads of light, which dance as they travel and trace their way through our vision, linking us and their source, and holding us in their beams. And with meanings that range from shuttling backwards and forwards to yielding, 'truckle' might hint at the play of darkness yielding to light, or at our yielding to the light as it greets us; or perhaps strands of light yield to the flicker of eyelashes as we open and close our eyes.

DAY 9: FRIDAY

For Hopkins, this candle indoors brings questions. Who sits in this indoors? Who is lit by this candle and what are they doing? ('By that window what task what fingers ply.') As he walks and wonders and questions, his heart is moved by the invisible souls whose candles he sees, 'a-wanting' and again 'a-wanting' the unknown 'Jessy or Jack' in their ordinary homes to be glorified by God – or to glorify God:

There God to aggrándise, God to glorify.—

With the line extending after 'glorify', it seems that Hopkins might go on to say more about what he wants; he might even slide into judging those he does not know. But he stops; and in the space between the octet and the sestet, there is a characteristic change of tone, perspective and mood. It is as if Hopkins suddenly realizes – or is reminded – that it is not for him to know or judge how those who take the trouble to light the candle and live in its glow are living their lives; how they know and share God.

He must look to another candle of another indoors to light his way to the God he wants to glorify. 'Come you indoors, come home,' we hear; whether this is his own call to himself or God's call to him, we may hear in these words both pity and urgency. The plea to 'come you indoors, come home' is a turn from one 'indoors' to another; from one hearth to another.

Why call for the glow of other lives to glorify God, when it is the light of our own heart we must 'mend first' to allow the 'vital candle' to burn brightly? It is within, says the poet, it is only within that the call to new life may be deeply heard. Then the tone seems to become more urgent, more self-questioning, as he asks, 'What hinders?' 'What stops you from attending to *your* candle indoors?' And in an echo of the 'trambeams' of soft, shuttling light from another candle indoors and the 'beam' that blinds us to ourselves in Matthew's Gospel,[25] we hear:

THE CANDLE INDOORS

> Are you beam-blind, yet to a fault
> In a neighbour deft-handed?

'Are you both "beam-blind" and "deft-handed"?' he asks himself. 'Slow to notice what lies within but quick to see ("deft-handed") others' faults?' In a final heartfelt cry (and with another allusion to Matthew's Gospel), Hopkins seems to confront himself with a heart-opening question:

> Are you that liar
> And, cast by conscience out, spendsavour salt?

To lose sight of the flame within, which needs tending, might also be to lose savour as the salt of the earth: salt and light both lost by averting our gaze from the candle that needs tending within. With its pity, struggle, beauty and self-questioning, 'The Candle Indoors' is a call to attend to the light we are gifted by God's grace, to ask ourselves the hard questions about what we turn away from, and to be willing to come home to the light of Christ that dwells within and which – during Lent, through our wilderness walk – we may discover shines more brightly.

> Come you indoors, come home; your fading fire
> Mend first and vital candle in close heart's vault.

Day 10

Saturday

God's Grandeur

The world is charged with the grandeur of God.
   It will flame out, like shining from shook foil;
   It gathers to a greatness, like the ooze of oil
Crushed. Why do men then now not reck his rod?
Generations have trod, have trod, have trod;
   And all is seared with trade; bleared, smeared with toil;
   And wears man's smudge and shares man's smell: the soil
Is bare now, nor can foot feel, being shod.

And for all this, nature is never spent;
   There lives the dearest freshness deep down things;
And though the last lights off the black West went
   Oh, morning, at the brown brink eastward, springs —
Because the Holy Ghost over the bent
   World broods with warm breast and with ah! bright wings.

Lent 1877 began mistily over North Wales. From Ash Wednesday on 14 February, chilly, cloudy and overcast weather rolled on day by day, with rain and high winds moving erratically across the land.[26] So it may be surprising that on the tenth day of Lent, Hopkins poured out, in buoyant, fresh and vivid language, a vision of the world transfigured by the glory of God streaming through the landscape, from the heights of the heavens to the depths of the earth.

Written a few months after 'The Wreck of the Deutschland' was rejected for publication,[27] it is as if, unleashed from the possibilities of gaining a wider audience, Hopkins felt able to give free rein to his quixotic, exquisitely crafted vision-in-verse of God's world. He had felt for some time the stirrings of his own poetic voice: the 'echo of a new rhythm ... haunting' him.[28] And if this first found expression in 'The Wreck', it appeared to reach maturity the following year. Now, discovering further poetic cadences in which he played with metre, stress and meaning-making, meaning-breaking language, Hopkins was developing a poetic register to reflect the irregular, bouncing, unpredictable pattern of ordinary speech rather than the epic framing of poetic language. This 'sprung rhythm' was not, he acknowledged, 'altogether new' as he saw 'hints of it in music, in nursery rhymes and popular jingles, in the poets themselves'.[29] However, Hopkins' approach of focusing on *stresses* in a line (with any number of unstressed syllables), when combined with his unique vision of seeing-into the inscape of a thing and sharing that, brought to birth a poetic form that was both old and new.

'God's Grandeur' seems to fall into three parts: each with its own sense and timbre; each with its own soundscape to help shape its meaning. In the opening four lines, the doors are flung wide to a vision of effervescent divine life. Words tumble out as Hopkins launches on his task to tell us that

> The world is charged with the grandeur of God.
>   It will flame out, like shining from shook foil;
>   It gathers to a greatness, like the ooze of oil
> Crushed. Why do men then now not reck his rod?

From the very outset, we are caught in a vision of the whole world crackling with light, as if a divine electric storm rakes the sky. Stress follows stress ('*char*ged', '*gran*deur of *God*') and seems to propel us forward, like the glory that will, says the poet, 'flame out', lighting up the sky 'like shining from shook foil'. This, said Hopkins in later years, was the kind of 'goldfoil' that gives off both a kind of sheet lightning and also forked lightning because of its 'dints and creasings': 'no other word' would do, he said, to convey God's crackling and overflowing presence.[30] And perhaps no other word could adequately convey the gold-leaf profligacy of God, which not only shimmers but also 'gathers to a greatness, like the ooze of oil / Crushed' as if to anoint and smooth the way of God's dynamic creation. Then the tone changes.

'Why do men then now not reck his rod?' asks the poet. And we are suddenly presented with the mystery of why we pay no heed to the one who gives us life and who sanctifies the most ordinary of places. With the multivalency of ancient-modern language, in 'reck his rod' we find resonances of 'heed' and 'reckoning'; of 'authority', of 'lightning rod'; and even of the Rood – the Cross of Christ. In these few words, we are invited to ponder why we ignore God's authority; why we are careless of God's vivid presence; why we take no heed for the sacrifice of Christ. We have lost touch with God's grandeur, we hear, as a new soundscape emerges:

> Generations have trod, have trod, have trod;
>   And all is seared with trade; bleared, smeared with toil;
>   And wears man's smudge and shares man's smell: the soil
> Is bare now, nor can foot feel, being shod.

Far from language that flares and propels us, we now find ourselves among the shuffling 'generations' who 'have trod, have trod, have trod' and who are no longer able to feel the ground beneath their feet ('nor can foot feel, being shod'). And between 'trod' and 'shod', echoing, rhyming words paint a picture of humanity as 'seared', 'bleared' and 'smeared'. We have, says the poet, become withered and lifeless, dimmed, dulled and diverted from God to our own concerns; we have overlaid God's world with ourselves, such that all we touch now seems to wear 'man's smudge' and share 'man's smell'. In this soundscape of repetition and echo and emphasis, deepened by internal rhymes and repeated 'ands', we join an emphatic march of shod feet trudging over 'bare soil'.

Then the tone shifts again; and with a new softness, the grandeur of God returns in resurrection glimmers.

And for all this, nature is never spent;
  There lives the dearest freshness deep down things;
And though the last lights off the black West went
  Oh, morning, at the brown brink eastward, springs —
Because the Holy Ghost over the bent
  World broods with warm breast and with ah! bright wings.

Though we may have covered God's earth with our own concerns, says Hopkins, though we may have lost touch with the ground beneath our feet, or become withered and dimmed, 'nature is never spent'. Beneath and within, 'there lives the dearest freshness deep down things'. In sounds more sibilant, more gentle and more lingering, we discover the persistence of God's life, always waiting to emerge. We discover the 'freshness' of new birth, which can no more be prevented than dawn and can no more be prevented than resurrection. Though the 'last lights off the black West' disappear at nightfall, this is only the precursor of new life, expressed in the heartfelt, heart-filling exclamation: 'Oh, morning, at the brown brink eastward, springs.' The 'bare soil' has become the 'brown brink' of earth as it births new life, in a resurrection nurtured into being by the mothering of God's Spirit,

Because the Holy Ghost over the bent
  World broods with warm breast and with ah! bright wings.

God's grandeur, it seems, is as much in 'the brown brink' – in the intimations of new life – as in the 'shining from shook foil'. It is in the un-losable, day-by-day resurrections and endless new births around us that we are reminded, in the searing, blearing and smearing of life, that 'nature is never spent'.

In the years after he wrote 'God's Grandeur', Hopkins discovered as much about the depletions of daily living – the blear, the smear and the smudge – as he knew of life's moment-by-moment resurrections. This was ahead of him. In the meantime, he left us this vision of God's grandeur, birthed in Lent 1877, which is as subtle and supple as it is explosive and intimate. It

DAY 10: SATURDAY

is a vision that may help us, on our Lenten journey, to allow life's 'dearest freshness' to shape us, so that we may see afresh the glory and the vividness of God's world. It may also allow our hearts to become prepared for the great resurrection that lies ahead of us at Easter, in the greatest expression of God's grandeur.

Day 11

Monday

In the Valley of the Elwy

I remember a house where all were good
  To me, God knows, deserving no such thing:
  Comforting smell breathed at very entering,
Fetched fresh, as I suppose, off some sweet wood.
That cordial air made those kind people a hood
  All over, as a bevy of eggs the mothering wing
  Will, or mild nights the new morsels of Spring:
Why, it seemed of course; seemed of right it should.

Lovely the woods, waters, meadows, combes, vales,
All the air things wear that build this world of Wales;
  Only the inmate does not correspond:
God, lover of souls, swaying considerate scales,
Complete thy creature dear O where it fails,
  Being mighty a master, being a father and fond.

In the 1860s, the photographer Francis Bedford captured a river under a canopy of trees. Showing the sun shimmering in a central flash of light, spilling across water and undergrowth, even in its monochrome form, the scene appears freshly green and golden. This is a spot along the River Elwy, just a few years before its canopied valley became for Hopkins an echo of the graceful canopy of love human and divine, within and over our dappled lives.

If we were, today, to track the flow of the Elwy through its covering canopies of woodland, waterfalls and caves, we might begin at its western rising, not far from the small town of Llanrwst, about 25 miles west of St Beuno's. If we were then to travel north-east, we would come to the village of Llangernyw, where the river first takes the name Elwy. From there, road and river appear to travel in concert, flowing north and east towards Llanfair Talhaiarn, where waterway and road part company. As the road strikes out for the North Wales coast, the ancient river continues its meandering journey eastwards through countryside and hamlets; it eventually turns towards the north and joins the River Clwyd on its journey to the sea, passing through St Asaph on the way. It is at this point that the river passes most closely to St Beuno's, less than four miles away. So it is possibly at this point, just about an hour's walk or so from his home, that Hopkins might have been most familiar with the river's flow, where he walked and fished, and which inspired 'In the Valley of the Elwy'.

Place was important for Hopkins – and *this* place was important. In the weeks leading up to his writing 'In the Valley of the Elwy' in May 1877, he wrote and shared a paper that explored the importance of place in the Ignatian Spiritual Exercises. Perhaps most tellingly, he underlined that the use of place may enable the one praying through the Exercises to be 'present in spirit at the scenes ... so that they may really act on him and he on them'.[31] 'In the Valley of the Elwy' seems to be a poem of such prayerful presence; it also offers us a glimpse of how a landscape can evoke a particular and unique experience, an instress, in which time and place, memory and faith fuse to bring about a textured experience of God's eternal mercy in the heart of our lives.

That this moment in the valley of the Elwy is here and now, not here and not now, is apparent from the outset of the poem. Its title tells us where we are; but then, curiously, we immediately find ourselves somewhere else:

> I remember a house where all were good
>   To me, God knows, deserving no such thing:
>   Comforting smell breathed at very entering,
> Fetched fresh, as I suppose, off some sweet wood.

In these first four lines, we find ourselves in a house instead of a valley: to be precise in the home of 'kind people', the Watsons, who lived on Shooters Hill.[32] Held within a careful rhyme scheme, words and sense flow across lines in a reflective murmuring that draws us into a memory poured out before us in this fluid place. 'All were good / To me,' remembers Hopkins, 'God knows, deserving no such thing.' At the heart of his memory, at the heart of 'In the Valley of the Elwy', is the grace of a gift undeserved, which simply arrives and is remembered in the 'comforting smell' of a welcoming fire, 'fetched fresh, as I suppose, off some sweet wood'. 'God knows,' says Hopkins; 'I suppose,' he echoes, drawing us deeper into his fluid reverie.

Place and place, time and time seem to flow together and rise to meet the poet. The shimmering memory of a home canopied by a hood of 'cordial air', casting a covering like a brooding bird holding her wing over her soon-to-hatch young, also reminds him of gentle temperate spring nights hovering over seasonal buds – the 'new morsels' of Spring. And all of this, we hear, feels entirely right: such comfort, such gentle and loving protection seems to be the most natural thing in the world.

> That cordial air made those kind people a hood
>   All over, as a bevy of eggs the mothering wing
>   Will, or mild nights the new morsels of Spring:
> Why, it seemed of course; seemed of right it should.

Then, as so often with a sonnet, the mood shifts from the octet to the sestet: we are lifted away from a moment of memory, into the present; into the beauty of the world of Wales, its 'woods, waters, meadows, combes and vales'. More than the woods, though, more than the combes and more than the vales, it is 'the air things wear' that marks the place Hopkins celebrates. Just as it was the 'cordial air' in Shooters Hill and the 'comforting smell ... / Fetched fresh ... off some sweet wood', it is the air itself that shapes his beloved Wales – his beloved Elwy Valley. So we are drawn into the spirit of place, quickened by the Spirit of grace:

DAY 11: MONDAY

Lovely the woods, waters, meadows, combes, vales,
All the air things wear that build this world of Wales;
   Only the inmate does not correspond:
God, lover of souls, swaying considerate scales,
Complete thy creature dear O where it fails,
   Being mighty a master, being a father and fond.

'Only the inmate does not correspond,' says the poet, wondering that in our undeserving state we should be gifted such life, sweetness and comfort: so generous, so profligate is the Giver. Hopkins' only response in this place of beauty, which casts our dappled nature into the shade, is to pray to the One who loves us even in our flawed state; to pray to 'God, lover of souls', who, 'swaying considerate scales', balances justice with mercy. This is a prayer for graceful assistance from the Giver of all graces, who is 'mighty a master, being a father and fond'; and whose goodness, made known in a graced place, blends with another memory of grace, goodness, sweetness and equally undeserved love.

Few poems of Hopkins carry such a gentle sense of consolation as 'In the Valley of the Elwy'. Here, there are no noisy miracles, no flashes of blue sparkling feather or ringing bird of prey; but there is a canopy of love and grace, within which it is safe to reflect in dappled sunlight on our dappled nature and look to a merciful God who knows all and loves all. With this, we may emerge (as Hopkins did just a few months later when he left St Beuno's) and enter the tremors of the world, nourished by the one who holds us in graceful self-giving; nourished by memories made and memories being born, forging – instressing – an interior landscape of love and grace, of kindness and mercy.

Day 12

Tuesday

I Wake and Feel

I wake and feel the fell of dark, not day.
What hours, O what black hours we have spent
This night! what sights you, heart, saw; ways you went!
And more must, in yet longer light's delay.

With witness I speak this. But where I say
Hours I mean years, mean life. And my lament
Is cries countless, cries like dead letters sent
To dearest him that lives alas! away.

I am gall, I am heartburn. God's most deep decree
Bitter would have me taste: my taste was me;
Bones built in me, flesh filled, blood brimmed the curse.

Selfyeast of spirit a dull dough sours. I see
The lost are like this, and their scourge to be
As I am mine, their sweating selves; but worse.

'I Wake and Feel' takes us into a world of wakefulness at the dead of night: those silent hours when the burdens of our hearts are amplified; our laments sharper; our doubts looming shadows seeping through bittersweet faith, at once beckoning us and leaving us adrift. This is a poem of profound humanity, from a poet and priest who has been carried to the heights of faithful exuberance and laboured through the pain of inner torment. If, in Lent, we hope to accompany Christ who knows all suffering, who has walked through wilderness and sat in a star-hovered Gethsemane, this poem might help us encounter him.

Only discovered after his death, 'I Wake and Feel' emerged in the season of Hopkins' 'Terrible Sonnets',[33] written around 1885, in the midst of his struggles with 'fits of sadness … which resemble madness' and a 'jaded and harassed mind'.[34] His muse became unpredictable, with verse sometimes arriving 'like inspirations unbidden and against my will'[35] or 'written in blood'.[36] Today and over the next two days, we shall follow three of these 'Terrible Sonnets' and explore the subtleties of their mood shifts and even intimations of grace.

Whether the fruit of sudden inspiration or of agonizing, painful birth, 'I Wake and Feel' tingles with the depth and authenticity of experience: a quality he craved in his writing. 'The worst fault a thing can have,' he wrote during this same year, was 'unreality'.[37] In this poem, we are plunged immediately into sleep-wrecking wakefulness, with the first opening of an eye onto the fierce cruelty of darkness instead of daylight. 'I wake and feel the fell of dark, not day,' says Hopkins in a line that echoes Dante's wilderness-wakening in a dark place. Then, almost immediately, 'I' becomes 'we' and we hear Hopkins' conversation at the dead of night with his own heart:

> What hours, O what black hours we have spent
> This night! what sights you, heart, saw; ways you went!
> And more must, in yet longer light's delay.

'Hours,' we hear. 'O what black hours,' Hopkins repeats, with an intensity that rolls across on to the next line ('we have spent / This night!'), lengthening time, and somehow blurring the states of sleep and wakefulness. He and his addressed-heart have, it seems, been separate and united in the 'sights' and 'ways' they have shared; they will together continue to experience their bruising sadness in the darkness before sunrise, in the time of 'light's delay'. With beats and stresses, echoes and alliteration that cause us to move, to stop or to linger ('in yet *long*er *light*'s de*lay*), these opening lines have drawn us into the very human experience of the inner wilderness that assails us in the darkness before dawn's light.

As the poem goes on, the inner struggle appears to take on a new quality, shifting from the pain of mere 'hours' to years; to a whole lifetime of emotional vagaries, brought back through this night's torment. Still more than this is the pain of silence: of a heart reaching out to God, only to receive no echo of acknowledgement of a 'lament', which is

> cries countless, cries like dead letters sent
> To dearest him that lives alas! away.

The poet's cry is to his 'dearest', his beloved but as yet unnamed God to whom he 'cries like dead letters'. In this allusion to the 'Dead Letter Office' (then part of the postal service, which handled misaddressed letters, launched on their way only to miss the mark), there is the hint that the poet's countless cries to God have gone astray; and so they sit in a void of miscommunication. But perhaps there is in this a distant glimmer of light in the 'black hours', because to send 'dead letters' to God is still to reach out in hope that the one who 'lives alas! away' still lives.

It may also be this distant glimpse of light that shapes the turn of the sonnet's final six lines, even though these lines are shot through with suffering and the crier in the night is still caught in the pain of isolation. Now looping back inwards from the dead letters flung outwards, Hopkins turns towards scouring self-reflection. 'I am gall,' he says, 'I am heartburn,' called to know his own bitter taste:

> God's most deep decree
> Bitter would have me taste: my taste was me;
> Bones built in me, flesh filled, blood brimmed the curse.
>
> Selfyeast of spirit a dull dough sours.

The ambivalence of these lines is striking. Perhaps Hopkins feels that the 'bitter taste' is part of who he is called to be in 'God's most deep decree', with a painful acknowledgement of his own mottled humanity. Or perhaps he feels it is he who, through his own 'selfyeast of spirit', sours the building blocks and the 'dull dough' of his life. Perhaps he hovers among myriad understandings of a life shaped both by agony and by the God who calls him even in the midst of agony. Finally, and in one last poetic turn, we are shown another glimpsed picture of Hopkins' churning reflections. 'I see,' he says,

> The lost are like this, and their scourge to be
> As I am mine, their sweating selves; but worse.

'The lost are like this,' he says, 'but worse.' In a moment of exhausted revelation, he seems to grasp that his agonized cry *is* agony; but it is not the cry of one lost to God. No matter how dark the night, how deep the suffering, such darkness, such suffering does not lose us to our God.

'I Wake and Feel' opens out for us the torment, isolation and self-doubt that can be part of any life, and that are all to be found in the Passion towards which we are travelling in Lent. As the Lenten journey goes on, we may draw closer to the depth of suffering borne by Christ. We may also draw closer to the realization that inner agony, no matter how sharp and life-shaping, does not lose us to God. Even in the dark of a Gethsemane night, even on a Golgotha afternoon as the sky darkens, we may know the 'fell of dark' and not be lost.

Day 13

Wednesday

Patience, Hard Thing

Patience, hard thing! the hard thing but to pray,
But bid for, Patience is! Patience who asks
Wants war, wants wounds; weary his times, his tasks;
To do without, take tosses, and obey.

Rare patience roots in these, and, these away,
Nowhere. Natural heart's ivy, Patience masks
Our ruins of wrecked past purpose. There she basks
Purple eyes and seas of liquid leaves all day.

We hear our hearts grate on themselves: it kills
To bruise them dearer. Yet the rebellious wills
Of us we do bid God bend to him even so.

And where is he who more and more distils
Delicious kindness?—He is patient. Patience fills
His crisp combs, and that comes those ways we know.

'Patience is a virtue, though it may often displease,' wrote the Middle English 'Pearl-poet' about Jonah's embattled call to teach in an unfamiliar city.[38] Four hundred years later, another English poet and teacher, newly arrived in an unfamiliar city, wrote 'Patience, hard thing!'

Gerard Manley Hopkins had arrived in Dublin on the cusp of Lent 1884 to begin his final posting as a teacher and academic. It was to span the last five years of his life. But if the posting brought stability after years of moving from place to place, so too did it bring years of desolation: fitful moods, sadness and ill-health; years of feeling exiled, 'jaded' and 'harassed'.[39] These were the years of his 'Terrible Sonnets', crying from out of the depths of his humanity to the God who called him.

It was in the midst of this time, in 1885, when peace was sorely lacking and patience tested for Hopkins, that 'Patience, Hard Thing' arrived. For a priest schooled in the Ignatian Spiritual Exercises, the virtue of patience would have been familiar from the eighth rule, which says that 'when one is in desolation, he should strive to persevere in patience', though this is difficult when 'vexations have overtaken him'. The call of this rule was to let the follower know that 'consolation will soon return', and that he was to draw on prayer, meditation and self-examination to help with forging patience.[40] What a hard thing this is, Hopkins tells us, in a poem that explores the difficulty, the challenge of finding so elusive, so demanding a quality as patience.

In 'Patience, Hard Thing', we are drawn through the search for a personified Patience in a sonnet in which words and lines bend back on themselves, invert and invite us into the tortuous and painful experience of seeking Patience when we are all but desolate; when we are weary and wounded, assailed by pains within and without.

> Patience, hard thing! the hard thing but to pray,
> But bid for, Patience is! Patience who asks
> Wants war, wants wounds; weary his times, his tasks;
> To do without, take tosses, and obey.

With language so pared down that meaning becomes fluid ('Patience, hard thing!' rather than 'Patience *is a* hard thing!'), the poem becomes both strangely emphatic and multivalent. Associations and possible meanings hover in the spaces between words, somehow hinting more deeply at the challenge of seeking this gift of patience in the midst of our deepest pains. Even the prayer needed for Patience is difficult: we hear, in emphatic,

echoing words running across lines, 'The hard thing is to pray /
But bid for, Patience is!'

To seek Patience, it seems, we need patience; and in seeking
Patience, we may find that our relationship with life's difficulties is laid bare in all its complexity. Perhaps the one seeking
Patience lacks ('*wants*') war and wounds, through the very act
of seeking. Or perhaps whoever seeks Patience paradoxically
desires ('*wants*') the war and wounds that trap us in familiarity and distract from the struggle for Patience, which is both
sought and rejected, as we tie ourselves in a knot of indecisive
spiritual yearning. We seek both God and to distract ourselves
from ourselves.

But Patience, we are told, takes root in the struggles – the
'tosses' – of life, whether wars or wounds; and as it comes into
being only when tested, without such struggles ('these away'),
Patience is 'Nowhere':

> Rare patience roots in these, and, these away,
> Nowhere. Natural heart's ivy, Patience masks
> Our ruins of wrecked past purpose. There she basks
> Purple eyes and seas of liquid leaves all day.

Patience, Hopkins tells us, is the 'Natural heart's ivy', reaching
into the cracks that open in life, whether fissure or crevasse;
and as on any ivy-clad building, the effect is of covering – of
'mask[ing]' – all the unevenness of life, the 'ruins of wrecked past
purpose', so that all becomes levelled out. All is held together
by kind, protective Patience, which 'basks', we are told, in a
seascape of leaves flowing through all the gulleys and breaks
and fissures of the heart; smoothing and holding together all
ravages, with the 'purple eyes' of its berries and healing quality
of its leaves. But ivy is also a curiously mixed image: it may
protect, but so too may it disguise and tease further open the
cracks and gulleys. This tendril-hold of Patience, this web for
grace and protector for wounds, may hold all and cover all;
but is this covering of life's wounds enough?

DAY 13: WEDNESDAY

For Hopkins, the answer seems to be to widen our vision and to surrender and receive as much as to seek. After the volta, the sonnet shifts and we are drawn away from the heartsore search for Patience; drawn away, too, from the turmoil of a virtue that is craved and costly, which may protect and may cover, but may also conceal cracks and crevices of lives rent apart. Now, the call is for balm because 'we hear our hearts grate on themselves: it kills / To bruise them dearer'.

> Yet the rebellious wills
> Of us we do bid God bend to him even so.
>
> And where is he who more and more distils
> Delicious kindness?—He is patient. Patience fills
> His crisp combs, and that comes those ways we know.

In all our turmoil, we hear, our prayer may finally be to 'bid God bend to him' our 'rebellious wills'. Rather than seeking Patience to withstand inner chaos, turmoil and desolation, the prayer may be to seek the one 'who more and more distils / Delicious kindness'; to seek the one who is not Patience but *is* patient. This is a call to seek the Giver of grace and gift; and as we do so, to discover the sweetness of the patience that is offered, as it 'fills his crisp combs': as nectar may be gathered from myriad ivy plants and overflow combs with sweetness and balm, to soothe and to heal.

Patience is a hard thing – and as Hopkins suggests, it may not be ours to grasp. Perhaps the final word in the search for patience, as we seek to live in its embrace, is the call to surrender ourselves to the one who is patient. It may only be then that the sweetness of God may gently salve the woundedness of our lives, in all our rawness and brokenness and in his 'delicious kindness' to us in both our consolation and our desolation.

Day 14

Thursday

My own heart let me more have pity on

My own heart let me more have pity on; let
Me live to my sad self hereafter kind,
Charitable; not live this tormented mind
With this tormented mind tormenting yet.

I cast for comfort I can no more get
By groping round my comfortless, than blind
Eyes in their dark can day or thirst can find
Thirst's all-in-all in all a world of wet.

Soul, self; come, poor Jackself, I do advise
You, jaded, let be; call off thoughts awhile
Elsewhere; leave comfort root-room; let joy size

At God knows when to God knows what; whose smile
's not wrung, see you; unforeseen times rather—as skies
Betweenpie mountains—lights a lovely mile.

When the sonnet we have come to know as 'My own heart let me more have pity on' was first published, it appeared as the last of four unnamed sonnets, printed on two sides facing each other. These four sonnets, wrote Hopkins' friend and publisher Bridges, were 'all written undated in a small hand on the two sides of a half-sheet of common sermon-paper, in the order in which they are here printed'. He guessed that they may have been the sonnets that had come to his friend 'unbidden and

DAY 14: THURSDAY

against [his] will' at a time of living with a 'continually jaded and harassed mind' in 1885.[41]

The placement of these four sonnets (two of which we have explored in recent days)[42] seems to tell a story. From the isolation of 'To Seem the Stranger' and the night-lament of 'I Wake and Feel', the sonnets seem to move towards an agonizing search for patience and God's balm in 'Patience, Hard Thing'. As the last of the four, 'My own heart let me more have pity on', seems to follow in the slipstream of 'Patience' as a vision of tenderness in the midst of torment, of comfort and self-directed compassion blending with the gift of the unpredictable, heart-changing love of God. Whether these poems, written on that 'half-sheet of common sermon-paper' do reflect a progression of moods over time, or reflect the many aspects of Hopkins at a certain time in his life, is hard to know. Yet 'My own heart let me more have pity on' seems to flicker with that same hope to be found in the 'delicious kindness' of God's healing balm towards the end of 'Patience, Hard Thing'.

In this season of hardship in Hopkins' life, 'My own heart let me more have pity on' hovers between the torment that he knew and profound compassion. It nudges us, too, towards a comfort and tenderness, as well as towards a moment for the heart to heal and search itself in the midst of a penitential, self-scouring season. Unusually in the 'Terrible Sonnets', we begin with the need for pity and compassion for the suffering heart: a theme emphasized in two inversions of language, which bring the heart into the foreground and stress the need for pity and kindness.

> My *own heart* let me more have *pity* on; let
> Me *live* to my *sad self* hereafter *kind*,
> Charitable; *not* live this tormented mind
> With this tormented mind tormenting yet.

This is somehow more than kind: it is 'hereafter kind' – as if we are at a point of resolution as we eavesdrop on a private plea or prayer – that the one suffering may 'hereafter' be kind to his 'sad self'. The time has come for deep compassion and to salve his sorrowed heart. And all is emphasized in stresses that roam across gently stretched vowels ('heart', 'pity', 'live', 'sad self' and 'kind'), with a sort of insistent conviction that the time for kindness has begun – but that this is costly for one who has known such inner pain. His plea is for his heart to have pity on a tormented mind; and the balance of 'let me live' with 'not live' draws out this pain, this hope:

> *not* live this tormented mind
> With this tormented mind tormenting yet.

It seems that only a repetition of his agonies can give full expression to 'this tormented mind / With this tormented mind tormenting yet'. Torment, torment, torment, we hear; and the octet goes on to describe the contours of a mind caught in its own traps, in its own limitations.

> I cast for comfort I can no more get
> By groping round my comfortless, than blind
> Eyes in their dark can day or thirst can find
> Thirst's all-in-all in all a world of wet.

'Groping round' in his comfortless state will not yield comfort any more than those unable to see can bring light to their world ('can day'); any more than the deepest thirst can be assuaged in a 'world of wet', when the need is for the living waters of 'thirst's all-in-all'. In this, we hear the agony of the fruitless and misguided search for what we want and need, but somehow miss, as the 'tormented mind' runs its course. Comfort, light and water: all needed, all available, all missed in the agonies of inner torment and in the very human ability to overlook the gift and the source of comfort, the source of light and 'thirst's all-in-all'.

Then, as the octet dies away, the volta opens with a new register. Let go of the torment, we seem to hear, in an echo of the opening line. But now we are taken further – beyond the nurture of our own heart's pity and beyond the realization that grasping after comfort will not secure it. Instead, we seem to be moved towards a depth of surrender to the beauty and kindness of God:

> Soul, self; come, poor Jackself, I do advise
> You, jaded, let be; call off thoughts awhile
> Elsewhere; leave comfort root-room; let joy size
>
> At God knows when to God knows what; whose smile
> 's not wrung, see you; unforeseen times rather—as skies
> Betweenpie mountains—lights a lovely mile.

As if drawing together the whole of him, Hopkins appeals first to his 'soul, self', then draws in his 'Jackself' – his ordinary, workaday, 'jaded' self – with an echo of how he described himself to Bridges.[43] '"Let be,"' he advises himself. 'Still your tormented mind ("call off thoughts") and, more importantly, "leave comfort root-room".' Rather than grasping comfortlessly after comfort and missing the mark, give comfort room to become embedded, to root itself and to grow. 'Let joy size,' we hear, too: let joy grow 'at God knows when to God knows what'. If there is a slight tone of frustration in this, there is also the deep recognition that God's time, God's hand are not to be forced. God's 'smile / 's not wrung, see you', we hear in languorous sounds that cross slowly from one line to another, drawing out a timing not our own but God's. This is the timing of the comforter, with whom we give 'comfort root-room', whose smile comes 'unforeseen times' rather than our bidding, and

>   as skies
> Betweenpie mountains—lights a lovely mile.

For Robert Bridges, who pondered the meaning of the curious 'betweenpie', these words conjured the 'brightly dappled' sky 'seen between dark mountains'.[44] This then, may be how God comes to us: unexpectedly; in the piebald beauty of blended shade and light, of desolation shot through with consolation, reaching across the 'lovely mile' of life's mountainous path. 'My own heart let me more have pity on; let / Me live to my sad self hereafter kind,' the poem began. It has drawn us through a plea for the heart's compassion and a need to surrender our own pains and torment; and it has drawn us towards an understanding that comfort *is* to be found, but not at our bidding. It is to be found in the God who smiles unbidden and who opens up to us a piebald vision of dappled light and grace.

Day 15

Friday

The Wreck of the Deutschland

To the happy memory of five Franciscan Nuns, exiles by the Falk Laws, drowned between midnight and morning of Dec. 7th, 1875

Part 1, Stanzas 1–5

      Thou mastering me
    God! giver of breath and bread;
  World's strand, sway of the sea;
    Lord of living and dead;
Thou hast bound bones & veins in me, fastened me flesh,
And after it almost unmade, what with dread,
    Thy doing: and dost thou touch me afresh?
Over again I feel thy finger and find thee.

      I did say yes
    O at lightning and lashed rod;
  Thou heardst me truer than tongue confess
    Thy terror, O Christ, O God;
Thou knowest the walls, altar and hour and night:
The swoon of a heart that the sweep and the hurl of
    thee trod
    Hard down with a horror of height:
And the midriff astrain with leaning of, laced with fire
  of stress.

THE WRECK OF THE DEUTSCHLAND (1)

        The frown of his face
      Before me, the hurtle of hell
    Behind, where, where was a, where was a place?
      I whirled out wings that spell
And fled with a fling of the heart to the heart of the Host.
  My heart, but you were dovewinged, I can tell,
    Carrier-witted, I am bold to boast,
To flash from the flame to the flame then, tower from the grace to the grace.

        I am soft sift
      In an hourglass—at the wall
    Fast, but mined with a motion, a drift,
      And it crowds and it combs to the fall;
I steady as a water in a well, to a poise, to a pane,
  But roped with, always, all the way down from the tall
    Fells or flanks of the voel, a vein
Of the gospel proffer, a pressure, a principle, Christ's gift.

        I kiss my hand
      To the stars, lovely-asunder
    Starlight, wafting him out of it; and
      Glow, glory in thunder;
Kiss my hand to the dappled-with-damson west:
Since, tho' he is under the world's splendour and wonder,
    His mystery must be instressed, stressed;
For I greet him the days I meet him, and bless when I understand.

The poet Hopkins, sleeping since 1868, was awakened in the winter of 1875 by tragedy. Early December that year was snow-covered and storm-struck; and as the winds rose and visibility dropped around the east coast of England,[45] the SS *Deutschland*, a ship bound from Germany to America, lost its bearings and foundered on the notoriously treacherous Kentish Knock sandbank to the east of the Thames.

    Among those lost overnight on 6 and 7 December were five

religious sisters who had been leaving their homeland in search of religious freedom. Now commemorated in an east London graveyard, they are also commemorated in Gerard Manley Hopkins' groundbreaking, two-part long poem, 'The Wreck of the Deutschland'. Much of the poem is dedicated to the wreck and the story of one of the lost sisters. But Part 1, covering the first ten stanzas, focuses on God: on the mystery and exhilaration, the challenge and the terror of a life caught up with God. We shall explore Part 1 over two reflections; and as Lent moves towards the Passion and beyond, we shall return to 'The Wreck' to explore just a few of its final stanzas.

The poem begins with a storm of passion and faith hurled into the heavens:

> Thou mastering me
> God! giver of breath and bread;
> World's strand, sway of the sea;
> Lord of living and dead;

Possibilities pour from these first few words, which may be prayer or yearning, praise or passion, or even a kind of rage towards the God who 'masters' him. 'You hold sway over me: teach me, set the direction of my heart and my life,' Hopkins seems to say to this 'mastering' God, who like a ship's master may chart a stormy or a peaceful course. From these Job-like words, the verse continues to ripple with scriptural echoes. God is the 'giver of breath and bread', creator and sustainer, recalling the daily bread of the Lord's prayer and eucharistic bread. It is God who shapes the contours of the world's shore (its 'strand'); and as 'sway of the sea', this 'Lord of living and dead' seems to *cause* and to *be* the movement of the waves that swallow the lost.

'Thou hast bound bones & veins in me, fastened me flesh,' Hopkins goes on, calling to mind the psalmist's cry to God: 'It was you who formed my inward parts; you knit me together in my mother's womb';[46] but in 'The Wreck', this is stretched. With God, says the poet, we can be 'unmade' as well as made;

formed and re-formed in the dance of drawing close to God, whose touch on our lives is never-ending:

> Thou hast bound bones & veins in me, fastened me flesh,
> And after it almost unmade, what with dread,
>   Thy doing: and dost thou touch me afresh?
> Over again I feel thy finger and find thee.

This passionate opening verse sets the scene for the whole poem. Opened out before us is the mystery of God who is our 'master' and beyond our knowing; One who shapes our living and our dying, who is both storm and harbour, and to whom we are bound even in the drownings of life. For Hopkins, this mystery is not a puzzle but an 'incomprehensible certainty',[47] rooted in the life, death and Resurrection of Christ, and drawing us on in faithful yearning. In 'The Wreck', it is also Hopkins' bounding, exhilarating sprung rhythm[48] that draws us on.

This rhythm powers the following verses in which Hopkins lays out before us the vibrant moves of the faithful heart: darting through peace and danger, and through call and choice. 'I did say yes,' we hear the poet say: 'yes' to this incomprehensible God of 'lightning and lashed rod' (stanza 2). And in return, he was heard 'truer than tongue confess / Thy terror, O Christ, O God': heard, perhaps, beyond his words and beyond his understanding.

We are carried along, as the poem unfolds, by language that is precise in its construction and impressionistic in its meaning; that catches us in the slipstream of a faith-filled soul on its all-consuming and inevitable journey of encounter with God. We hear about the 'swoon of a heart' and the 'sweep and hurl' of God (stanza 2) in echoing sounds that draw us into the heart's quest and the vigorous draw of God. We hear of the physicality of faith, of one 'astrain with the leaning of, laced with fire of stress' (stanza 2); and we hear of one hemmed-in before and behind by the leading and pursuing God ('the frown of his face / Before me, the hurtle of hell / behind'), leading to the poet's breathless cry in the third verse: 'Where, where was a,

DAY 15: FRIDAY

where was a place?' A place of what? Safety perhaps or peace? Or maybe it is a place at the eye of the storm of life with God, where in surrender, peace may be found – beyond the noise – at the very heart of the mystery of God: 'at the heart of the Host', in a multivalent placè of sanctuary. Here perhaps our heart is 'dovewinged', filled with the Spirit of God and with the knowledge of God ('carrier-witted'), who carries the soul in flight.

Towards the end of these first five verses, the mood and sounds change. 'I am soft sift / In an hourglass', Hopkins begins in the fourth verse, with echoes of the Ash Wednesday acknowledgement that we are dust. In the heart of the storms, the fight and bustle of life, and in the depths of our embattled following, it seems that there may be a kind of peace in knowing our surrendered mortality as sand in an hourglass, gently falling. Yet as life slips along its mortal path, 'Christ's gift' is always made present to us, in wellsprings from the fells and the *voel* ('bare hill' in Welsh), which hold out to us 'a vein / of the gospel', a 'pressure, a principle, Christ's gift'.

The closing stanza of this first reflection on 'The Wreck' is as gentle as the first was embattled and stormy. The gentle sibilants of its opening words ('I kiss my hand / To the stars, lovely-asunder / Starlight') call to mind a scattering, scudding light across the heavens, which 'wafts' God through the skies in beauty and the 'glory of thunder'. 'Kiss my hand', repeats the poet; this time, he brings before us the gently stippling sound of the 'dappled-with-damson west' and the beauty of a rose sunset, filled with the richness of Hopkins' dappled world in which may be discovered the 'splendour and wonder' of God.

Worship pours from this fifth verse, with its shade and light, speed and stillness: all bearing witness to the glories of God. More than this, such glory, such 'mystery must be instressed, stressed'. We are called to catch, meet, take into ourselves such glory; to be shaped and formed by it; and so move from simply greeting God to blessing God:

> For I greet him the days I meet him, and bless when
>   I understand.

Day 16

Saturday

The Wreck of the Deutschland

Part 1, Stanzas 6–10

    Not out of his bliss
    Springs the stress felt
  Nor first from heaven (and few know this)
    Swings the stroke dealt—
Stroke and a stress that stars and storms deliver,
That guilt is hushed by, hearts are flushed by and melt—
  But it rides time like riding a river
(And here the faithful waver, the faithless fable and miss).

    It dates from day
    Of his going in Galilee;
  Warm-laid grave of a womb-life grey;
    Manger, maiden's knee;
The dense and the driven Passion, and frightful sweat;
Thence the discharge of it, there its swelling to be,
  Though felt before, though in high flood yet—
What none would have known of it, only the heart, being hard at bay,

    Is out with it! Oh,
    We lash with the best or worst
  Word last! How a lush-kept plush-capped sloe
    Will, mouthed to flesh-burst,
Gush!—flush the man, the being with it, sour or sweet,

DAY 16: SATURDAY

> Brim, in a flash, full!—Hither then, last or first,
>   To hero of Calvary, Christ's feet—
> Never ask if meaning it, wanting it, warned of it—men go.
>
>   Be adored among men,
>   God, three-numberéd form;
>   Wring thy rebel, dogged in den,
>   Man's malice, with wrecking and storm.
>   Beyond saying sweet, past telling of tongue,
>   Thou art lightning and love, I found it, a winter and warm;
>   Father and fondler of heart thou hast wrung:
> Hast thy dark descending and most art merciful then.
>
>   With an anvil-ding
>   And with fire in him forge thy will
>   Or rather, rather then, stealing as Spring
>   Through him, melt him but master him still:
>   Whether at once, as once at a crash Paul,
>   Or as Austin, a lingering-out swéet skíll,
>   Make mercy in all of us, out of us all
> Mastery, but be adored, but be adored King.

We find ourselves at a turn in 'The Wreck of the Deutschland'. After a moment of seeming stillness at the end of stanza 5, Hopkins turns to ponder the mystery of Christ, using richly impressionistic language and an echoing soundscape, which seem to break through usual poetic cadences and call out of us the ability to 'instress' this great mystery.

But if we think we know the contours of this mystery to be 'instressed, stressed', we may be mistaken. It does not emerge from heaven or from a state of bliss, we are told, in simple strong sibilant sounds ('bliss', 'springs', 'stress', 'swings', 'stroke', 'stars', 'storms') which carry us swiftly through the verse towards new understandings. No, the source of the mystery that 'stars and storms deliver', that quietens our guilt and melts our hearts, emerges from something else entirely. This mystery 'rides time like a river,' we hear, in languorous, emphatic words, as the Incarnate One is gradually brought before us, seeming to ride with us in and out of earthly time.

The heart of this mystery, then, is rooted in the life of Christ; it dates from 'his going in Galilee'. In a swift soundscape of kenning words and alliteration, the poet brings before us the earthly life and death of Christ:

> Warm-laid grave of a womb-life grey;
> Manger, maiden's knee;

Through the allusive economy of 'warm-laid grave of a womb-life grey' and 'manger, maiden's knee', we may find images of Christ with his mother dancing before us: from a nativity, with the infant Christ laid on his mother's knee, to a pietà, with the crucified Christ cradled by his mourning mother. Or perhaps what comes to mind is how mixed human life can be: both 'warm-laid grave' and 'womb-life grey'. But the poem moves quickly on and 'the dense and the driven Passion' is brought before us, sounding out in repetitive hammering Ds the driven nails of the crucifixion; and then the 'frightful sweat', as of terror or agony or fever, before release. But this release – this 'discharge' – may also be the release into God's world of the divine life, which is still in 'high flood' among us, flooding through time just as Hopkins' words flood across verses:

> The dense and the driven Passion, and frightful sweat;
> Thence the discharge of it, there its swelling to be,
>   Though felt before, though in high flood yet—
> What none would have known of it, only the heart, being hard at bay,
>
>   Is out with it!

In a flow of sounds and images, ideas and impressions, Hopkins has shown us the Incarnation and the Passion and the mystery of God flowing through the world. Impressions of how we might instress this mystery occupy much of the next verse, at the centre of which is the 'lush-kept, plush-capped sloe': that slightly bloomed, sharp autumn berry. The experience of God breaking into our life, Hopkins suggests, can be as overwhelming, intense and all-consuming as the taste of sloe-juice from a ripe berry; it fills us, sweet and sour, so we are 'in a flash, full!' 'O taste and see that the LORD is good,' we might hear the psalmist say,[49] in this experience that holds fast to us and fills us – whether we are at our 'best or worst' – and later, as we hurry 'last or first', to the 'hero of Calvary, Christ's feet'. 'Never ask if meaning it, wanting it, warned of it—men go,' says Hopkins: we cannot help but bring ourselves to the one who fills our lives and who calls us out of the heart of mystery.

The intensity of Part 1 abates; in stanza 9, Hopkins turns, in simpler, faith-filled, devotional language, to an adoration of the one who meets us in our humanity. 'Be adored among men,' he begins as in prayer, 'and draw rebellious, contrary, "dogged" humanity towards you':

> Wring thy rebel, dogged in den,
>   Man's malice, with wrecking and storm.

We seem to hear in these lines the 'wrecking and storm' of which we are capable in our 'malice'; but so too may we hear intimations of the story of the wreck to come. We may even discern the poet's plea for God to draw us to him, through life's 'wrecking and storm', with a sense that the wrecks of life in which we find ourselves may also be places of grace in which we are drawn towards God. After all, as Hopkins goes on to say:

> Thou art lightning and love, I found it, a winter and warm;
>   Father and fondler of heart thou hast wrung:
> Hast thy dark descending and most art merciful then.

God is, says Hopkins, all things: 'lightning and love'; he is cold and heat; and he is stern Father and the heart's tender carer. With God, he suggests, darkness and mercy blend in all the dappling of life.

THE WRECK OF THE DEUTSCHLAND (2)

Hopkins ends Part 1 with a call for God to weave through our lives and melt our hearts, whether as a smith in a forge shaping intransigent metal or 'stealing as Spring' through our lives. And whether we instress the mystery of God 'at once, as once at a crash Paul' did on the road to Damascus, or gradually as a 'lingering-out swéet skill', as in the life of St Augustine, the plea is for mercy and mastery in the lives of all. But above all, his plea is for God to be adored:

> Make mercy in all of us, out of us all
> Mastery, but be adored, but be adored King.

Mercy, mastery, worship and mystery lie at the heart of Part 1 of this great poem. By its end, we have been invited into that unfathomable blend of grace and call, of storm and peace, which reaches into all faithful lives and which is to be found at the mysterious heart of the Passion ahead.

Day 17

Monday

The Windhover

To Christ our Lord
I caught this morning morning's minion, king-
    dom of daylight's dauphin, dapple-dawn-drawn Falcon,
        in his riding
    Of the rolling level underneath him steady air, and striding
High there, how he rung upon the rein of a wimpling wing
In his ecstasy! then off, off forth on swing,
    As a skate's heel sweeps smooth on a bow-bend: the hurl
        and gliding
    Rebuffed the big wind. My heart in hiding
Stirred for a bird, — the achieve of, the mastery of the thing!

Brute beauty and valour and act, oh, air, pride, plume, here
    Buckle! AND the fire that breaks from thee then, a billion
Times told lovelier, more dangerous, O my chevalier!

    No wonder of it: shéer plod makes plough down sillion
Shine, and blue-bleak embers, ah my dear,
    Fall, gall themselves, and gash gold-vermilion.

Two years after he wrote 'The Windhover', Hopkins famously told his friend Bridges that he thought it was 'the best thing I ever wrote'.[50] Written in the late spring of 1877, 'The Windhover' captures the moment when, walking across the hillsides around St Beuno's,[51] Hopkins was transported by the vision of a proud, bright, air-swooping bird, which, under the poet's gaze, was transformed into a knight, a king-son, a skater, a master of air, fire and earth – and which transformed the seer in the looking. 'What you look at hard', Hopkins had written in his journal in the spring of 1871, 'seems to look hard at you.'

It is this depth of seeing, this gaze, that seems to bring 'The Windhover' into vivid life. As we linger over this bright world and allow our own gaze to follow the poet's, we may also encounter the breath-robbing beauty of the bird and be taken into its flashing power, towards the 'gash gold-vermilion' of a Christ-filled world. 'The Windhover' was written at the height of Hopkins' poetic rebirth. The muse had returned and he was giving voice to new sprung rhythm:[52] playing with metre and stress; lashing words together to forge new meaning; and drawing on the complex consonant chime of Welsh verse – 'what they call *cynghanedd*', as he wrote in 1878.[53] Here was a poetic register shaped by the old and the new, by his ability to perceive and receive the Christ-ness of a thing, and by sharing the bouncing, unpredictable pattern of ordinary speech.

Rooted in this particular time of Hopkins' life, 'The Windhover' sits at an axis point in the poet's rare and rich spiritual imagination. Here is a poem that seems to reflect the creative outpouring of a gift held in abeyance and of a faith fired by imagination, yet still shot through with the flickering fear of poetic pride – no matter how carefully husbanded his gift and his calling. A few years after writing 'The Windhover', he added the now famous dedication 'To Christ our Lord', as if to offer afresh to Christ his creative, poetic gifts and to underline his view that the 'end ... purpose ... purport' and 'meaning' of the world 'is God' and its 'life or work to name and praise him'.[54]

Here in 'The Windhover' is the intense experience of seeing deeply into God's world in the Christ-given essence of a dawn-hovering bird of prey; so deeply that the poet takes it into himself and is transformed. He sees the bird's 'inscape' and 'instresses' it – and opens for us a vision of resurrected life at the heart of the world.

The poem's hurried, almost snatched opening ('I *caught* this morning'), with its immediate repetition of 'morning' and

DAY 17: MONDAY

division of 'king-dom' across two lines, arrests our attention straight away, just as the bird bursts into life for the poet. Here are speed and fluidity drawn in two lines, as if we, too, are caught up with a bird in flight; as if we, too, feel the thud of air vibrating under the downward beat of powerful wings, teased out in a repeated, insistent D:

> I caught this morning morning's minion, king-
>   dom of daylight's dauphin, dapple-dawn-drawn Falcon,
>   in his riding
>   Of the rolling level underneath him steady air, and striding
> High there.

If the sound of the poem figures-forth the speed and power of the bird, the words themselves draw a picture of regal beauty and courtly bonds. This is 'morning's minion', a beloved favourite[55] and follower of the dawn-light; this is 'daylight's dauphin', the royal son of the morning sun: 'dapple-dawn-drawn', reflecting and describing the patterning, patched light of daybreak as the bird 'rid[es] / ... the rolling level underneath'. A regal, son-of-a-king Falcon, bright in the morning air, both itself and more than itself: conjuring for us, in its God-given splendour, the glory of that other Son-of-a-king to whom the poem is dedicated.

From here, the bird circles around a central axis, swooping and rising to meet the sky. Air-bound falconry and earth-bound skating now come together in a patterning of image and sound to show us the skimming, rotating flight upwards of the windhover. It circles on the tip of its rippling ('wimpling') wing, straining on currents of air that bring both freedom and constraint. Then it is freed from the circling air as it rises; and 'then off, off forth on swing', with an angle and force – which bring to mind 'a skate's heel' – as it 'sweeps smooth on a bowbend', biting at such an angle that the skater turns and glides.

This is the natural glory of the bird in flight, which the poet 'caught'– grasped – in a moment and which we can now grasp through a patterning of sounds and pictures. The poet 'caught' the windhover 'in his riding ... and striding ... how he rung upon the rein ... then off ... as a skate's heel sweeps ... and gliding / Rebuffed the big wind'. This is a bird both free and shaped by the natural world; both utterly itself and shot through with a glory that takes it beyond itself. So much so, says Hopkins that:

> My heart in hiding
> Stirred for a bird, – the achieve of, the mastery of the thing!

We may ponder over Hopkins' 'heart in hiding'. Perhaps in the windhover he glimpses a fresh freedom beyond any carefully guarded heart. Perhaps momentarily, as he glimpses the freedom, unselfconsciousness and courage to ride the currents of life with vigour, he is lifted out of callings that are both weighty and life-giving.

Then the poem turns. Hopkins sees in the windhover strength and courage in its 'brute beauty and valour'; but it is as if we are also shown, in the slipping and sliding 'act, oh, air, pride, plume, here / Buckle!', what happens as the bird is wind-tossed or as it surrenders to the buffeting currents. It 'buckles'; but whether this 'buckles' suggests it is crumpling under the wind's force or 'buckling-up', drawing all its strength together, the windhover now seems to flash into new life and return stronger than ever:

> Brute beauty and valour and act, oh, air, pride, plume, here
> Buckle! AND the fire that breaks from thee then, a billion
> Times told lovelier, more dangerous, O my chevalier!

Hopkins' emphatic 'AND' somehow amplifies that this is strength born in wind-tossed vulnerability. There is buckling (perhaps collapsing, perhaps girding) *and* there is the 'fire that breaks' forth in the buckling. The windhover, now 'a billion / Times told lovelier, more dangerous', is shot through with resurrection life, more beautiful, 'more dangerous' than before; buckling, broken but bursting with the fire of new life. To gaze at the windhover at this moment is to see the world become a place of resurrected life, even in the depths of the earth – even in dying embers:

> No wonder of it: shéer plod makes plough down sillion
> Shine, and blue-bleak embers, ah my dear,
>   Fall, gall themselves, and gash gold-vermilion.

Even the 'shéer plod' of daily existence can bring new life: the plough is burnished to a shine in performing its ordinary, necessary action of turning earth; and the furrows ('sillion'), which will hold seed, point to the quickening that will come. Even embers that are all but dead ('blue-bleak') will 'gash gold-vermilion' if they fall and break open. There is life in the depths of the earth; there is fire in ash.

In gazing upon the windhover, Hopkins captured a vision that may, all these years later, carry us through Lent: that journey towards the mystery of triumph in darkness. It is a vision of the world shot through with the light, beauty, daring, surrender, brightness and life of Christ, even in life's buffetings and even for hearts in hiding. It is a vision of resurrected life in which the ash, which marked Lent's beginning, points towards the 'gash gold-vermilion' of a Christ-filled world.

Day 18

Tuesday

Hurrahing in Harvest

Summer ends now; now, barbarous in beauty, the stooks rise
Around; up above, what wind-walks! what lovely behaviour
Of silk-sack clouds! has wilder,
Meal-drift moulded ever and melted across skies?

I walk, I lift up, I lift up heart, eyes,
Down all that glory in the heavens to glean our Saviour;
And, éyes, heárt, what looks, what lips yet gave you a
Rapturous love's greeting of realer, of rounder replies?

And the azurous hung hills are his world-wielding shoulder
Majestic—as a stallion stalwart, very-violet-sweet!—
These things, these things were here and but the beholder
Wanting; which two when they once meet,
The heart rears wings bold and bolder
And hurls for him, O half hurls earth for him off under
   his feet.

It is early September 1877. Gerard Manley Hopkins has spent the day fishing and turns towards home, St Beuno's. The late summer, early autumn landscape opens up before him in heathered-hills, tinged blue in the distance by the sky's reflection and overlaid with a pillow of clouds. The fertile lowlands of the Vale of Clwyd, through which the Elwy steers its course, show the signs of harvest-tide activity, and Hopkins is inspired. Out of 'half an hour of extreme enthusiasm as I walked home alone one day from fishing in the Elwy',[56] he later told his friend Bridges, the 'Hurrahing Sonnet' was born.

The 'extreme enthusiasm' he experienced floods through this poem of rejoicing ('hurrahing') in the harvest. Hopkins shares with us the inscape of this created-and-worked landscape, which seems to be sentient as well as alive; a beholder as much as beheld and somehow catching us up in the body of Christ. To linger over the swooping movement of 'Hurrahing in Harvest', its resonances and echoes, may be to open up a poetic landscape as redolent with God as the landscape that so touched Hopkins on that long-ago afternoon.

'Summer ends now,' Hopkins begins emphatically, bringing us into the present of that moment and inviting us into the experience of that heady day of seeing the signs of the year's turning. 'Barbarous in beauty,' we hear, with all the associations of strangeness and sharpness, 'the stooks rise / Around', as if suddenly the landscape is transformed by sheaves gradually standing upright, waiting between harvesting and storing; preparing for their transformation from crop to food. This is a landscape on the move as the year turns from summer to autumn.

There is movement, too, in the sky, where the airily kenning-expressed 'wind-walks' (the clouds) 'behave' as if shaping and moving of their own volition.

> up above, what wind-walks! what lovely behaviour
> Of silk-sack clouds! has wilder,
> Meal-drift moulded ever and melted across skies?

Billowing like silken fabric – filling with air and collapsing like sacks that have caught the breeze – these are clouds that beg the poet's question: have clouds, like the powdery 'meal-drift' from milling, ever formed and dissolved like this as they chase across the sky, in a movement of the heavens on the evening breeze? The wonder is clear in the language that follows their 'lovely behaviour'; that tumbles through sounds which slip ('silk-sack') and billow ('wilder'), condense ('meal-drift moulded') and disperse ('melted').

Hopkins responds to this heavenly, earthly movement as if to the emerging vision of God at the heart of the landscape. 'I walk, I lift up, I lift up heart, eyes,' he says, emphatic in his repetition, looking up, casting up all that is in him. In this echo of the call to 'lift up our hearts' at the beginning of the Eucharist, it as if the poet, and we, are called towards a sacramental moment of transforming presence:

> I walk, I lift up, I lift up heart, eyes,
> Down all that glory in the heavens to glean our Saviour;
> And, éyes, heárt, what looks, what lips yet gave you a
> Rapturous love's greeting of realer, of rounder replies?

The moment continues and Hopkins 'looks down all that glory', down the ages, down the valley and down through the story of God-with-us to 'glean': to catch sight of our Saviour in the gleanings of the harvest; to see all that is being transformed in this time of transforming crop to food. In this moment of knowing and sharing the body of Christ, we seem to shimmer between worlds; and even more so when it suddenly seems that we could be gazing on God or God gazing on us. With the 'I' now absent, Hopkins may be addressing his *own* uplifted 'éyes, heárt' to ask if they have ever beheld so rapturous and authentic a vision of God's love. Or perhaps he is asking what 'looks, what lips' have ever offered so 'rapturous' a 'love's greeting' to *him*.

We might find ourselves moving between perspectives, helped by the slackening pace of these lines, which causes us to pause. Commas, stresses and repetitions all slow our lifted-up hearts and minds. Even the word 'rapturous' has a roundness and wonder to it that causes us to hesitate just before speaking it, giving the sound-echo of 'Saviour' and 'gave you a' more space and resonance.

The sense of wonder continues across the break between the sonnet's first eight and final six lines, as if we move towards a deepening of the vision already shared. From the place of transformation, the croplands of 'barbarous' stooks, Hopkins' eyes (and our eyes through him) have drifted upwards and along the wide view towards the 'azurous hung hills', blue with the sky's reflection and 'very-violet-sweet' with the tinge of heather. All is somehow now transformed into the 'world-wielding shoulder' of Christ, bearing, carrying all things:

> And the azurous hung hills are his world-wielding shoulder
> Majestic—as a stallion stalwart, very-violet-sweet!—
> These things, these things were here and but the beholder
> Wanting; which two when they once meet,
> The heart rears wings bold and bolder
> And hurls for him, O half hurls earth for him off under
>   his feet.

Then, suddenly we again seem to move from perspective to perspective: 'these things, these things were here and but the beholder / Wanting' we are told. It seems that these things *have always* been here but without a 'beholder', who may be the face of God 'wanting', lacking, yearning for humanity in the spare landscape. Or are *we* the beholders lacking, yearning for the face of God that may emerge in a moment such as this? Whatever the perspective, 'when they once meet' the heart rises to meet God present in the landscape 'and hurls for him, O half hurls earth for him off under his feet', in an outpouring of longing and devotion towards the one who catches us all up in creative love.

'Hurrahing in Harvest' captures a moment in the year of transformation, when the crops of the worked earth remind us of God, who is with us in transformation and known to us in the gift of transformed bread. If Lent is not harvest-time, it is nevertheless a time of harvest. It is a time of gathering in and winnowing and allowing the chaff of life to be sifted and to fall as we discover ourselves as creatures of God: beholding and beheld by our creator and caught up in the body of Christ.

Day 19

Wednesday

Felix Randal

Felix Randal the farrier, O is he dead then? my duty all ended,
Who have watched his mould of man, big-boned and
  hardy-handsome
Pining, pining, till time when reason rambled in it, and some
Fatal four disorders, fleshed there, all contended?

Sickness broke him. Impatient, he cursed at first, but mended
Being anointed and all; though a heavenlier heart began some
Months earlier, since I had our sweet reprieve and ransom
Tendered to him. Ah well, God rest him all road ever
  he offended!

This seeing the sick endears them to us, us too it endears.
My tongue had taught thee comfort, touch had quenched
  thy tears,
Thy tears that touched my heart, child, Felix, poor
  Felix Randal;

How far from then forethought of, all thy more boisterous
  years,
When thou at the random grim forge, powerful amidst peers,
Didst fettle for the great grey drayhorse his bright and
  battering sandal!

In April 1880, the year in which Liverpool became a city, a young man named Felix Spencer died of tuberculosis. A blacksmith from a young age, he lived in that inner city's industrial heartland. When his brief life ended, within a stone's throw of St Francis Xavier where Hopkins was serving, Felix Spencer was immortalized in a poem in which he became Felix Randal.

Arriving to serve here in 1879, Hopkins had been struck, as he so often was, by the grime-blasted poverty of life in the 'gloomy', 'museless' and 'wretched' industrial towns.[57] And yet in the narrowed, harrowed lives of city dwellers, Hopkins discovered a resilience of faith for which he had a profound respect: 'Our flock are fervent. I have not seen their equal,' he said of his parishioners in another industrial town.[58]

The poet in Hopkins lamented a 'museless' place; the priest cared deeply for the straightened life of a man robbed of vigour and drawn towards an early death. And so 'Felix Randal' emerged in all its poignant intensity and richly blended emotional landscape. For George Orwell, this was 'the best short poem in the language'; for others, Hopkins' use of local dialect seemed a little patronizing.[59] Perhaps the poem's ability to draw out such different reactions reflects the struggle of a poet-priest lost in an alien landscape, filled with a difficult-to-express sorrow, and caught up in the dappled blend of grace and gift at the heart of life's wildernesses.

From its opening line, the poem brings together the formal and informal, tenderness and distance, mortality and eternity:

Felix Randal the farrier, O is he dead then? my duty all ended,
Who have watched his mould of man, big-boned and
   hardy-handsome
Pining, pining, till time when reason rambled in it, and some
Fatal four disorders, fleshed there, all contended?

There is a strange, apparent casualness in the words 'O is he dead then?' But this could equally be a sigh of sadness as the priest-poet reflects on the finality of his care in life for a man 'big-boned and hardy-handsome', whose diminished end (expressed in the dying fall 'pining, pining') brought confusion in its wake ('reason rambled') and the dis-ease of some 'fatal four disorders, fleshed there'. In this alliterative dance, we find echoes of the ancient understanding of blend and balance in the four humours or temperaments; but in Felix, the harmony is lost and his life is lost.

And then the poem changes direction. After rehearsing the pain of tragic death, we find unfolded the story of a soul toiling through illness and discovering grace. Felix is a man 'broken' by sickness, who 'curse[s] at first' but who finally finds comfort. And we discover, in a series of alliterations ('anointed and all', 'heavenlier heart', 'reprieve and ransom'), that Felix's experience of God has been crackling into life even before his illness claimed him; even before the sacramental comfort of being anointed:

> a heavenlier heart began some
> Months earlier, since I had our sweet reprieve and ransom
> Tendered to him. Ah well, God rest him all road ever
>   he offended!

In just a few lines, then, we have travelled with Felix through his wilderness journey of fear of death, and his turning towards God, while the depths of illness were beginning to lay claim upon him. And in the midst of this, a voice breaks through, which sounds less like Hopkins and more colloquial; a voice that seems to draw us, if uncomfortably, towards the inner experience of the one suffering and finding peace and forgiveness. Felix is 'anointed and all'; and the plea that 'God rest him all road ever he offended' hints at the poet's deep desire to honour this man's life and death. Perhaps there is linguistic clumsiness here; but there is, too, a condensed poignancy to these lines – in these words – that lays before us sorrow and death, affection and respect, hope and new life.

This blend continues to unfold as the sonnet moves towards the mood-deepening sestet. There is, we are told, a growing of love in walking alongside others in their suffering; and the sense that this love is reciprocal is heightened by the language, which is echoing and inverted; inverted and echoing to show the sharing of priest and parishioner, one with another:

> This seeing the sick endears them to us, us too it endears.
> My tongue had taught thee comfort, touch had quenched
>   thy tears,
> Thy tears that touched my heart, child, Felix, poor
>   Felix Randal.

In the final lines, Felix seems to move back in time and beyond time. We circle back to see the young Felix in the prime of his life, in the shimmering picture of a man in his 'boisterous years'. And then he becomes a kind of composite figure: he is poor Felix Randal, a man of his own time and place, who 'fettle[s] for the great grey drayhorse' and who could not have foreseen what was to come. But he is also somehow rooted in an ancient landscape of the forge, 'powerful amidst peers', with the beat and timbre of Anglo-Saxon verse and, like a smith of ancient times, flashing light as he strikes and fits the 'bright and battering sandal' of the horseshoe.

We part company with Felix, with a vision of him in his prime, caught in time and eternity. And in saying goodbye to him, we may find ourselves with a blend of emotions, ranging from sorrow to celebration; from the pain of living in hardship to the intense and poignant richness of life while it can be lived, as well as to the glory of discovering God in the midst of life's hardships. 'Felix Randal' – this poem of life and life's departing, of grief and memory, of loss and redemption – is also a poem of compassion and deep humanity. It may draw us into the mystery of death in life and closer to God as we embrace our earth-bound horizon and look to our risen life.

It is a poem to accompany us in our own Lenten wilderness, with hearts open to being touched and shaped by the grace of God through our losses and discoveries.

Day 20

Thursday

As Kingfishers Catch Fire

As kingfishers catch fire, dragonflies draw flame;
   As tumbled over rim in roundy wells
   Stones ring; like each tucked string tells, each hung bell's
Bow swung finds tongue to fling out broad its name;
Each mortal thing does one thing and the same:
   Deals out that being indoors each one dwells;
   Selves — goes itself; *myself* it speaks and spells,
Crying *Whát I dó is me: for that I came.*

I say móre: the just man justices;
   Keeps grace: thát keeps all his goings graces;
Acts in God's eye what in God's eye he is —
   Chríst — for Christ plays in ten thousand places,
Lovely in limbs, and lovely in eyes not his
   To the Father through the features of men's faces.

From the beginning of the sonnet we have come to know as 'As Kingfishers Catch Fire', we are drawn into an explosive, expansive and particular world of God-with-us at the very heart of the creation.

Written in 1877, during that time of poetic flourishing when Hopkins was at St Beuno's and the world came alive in its graced beauty, this sonnet gifts us a vision of Christ investing all things, with their unique footprint, heartbeat and texture, from the infinitesimally small and the inanimate to the quickened human eye and heart. For Hopkins, there was no thing or place or person that fell beyond the presence of Christ, who calls all things into being in their uniqueness and individuality: their inscape, that unique inner landscape which blends self and identity, calling and purpose.

'As Kingfishers Catch Fire' is a celebration of this 'inscape', that Christ-gifted identity at the heart of all things, which can be glimpsed, apprehended, experienced by another; instressed by another. This was a deeply personal way of seeing the world, which Hopkins found echoed in the vision and theology of the twelfth-century Franciscan friar John Duns Scotus, whom the poet delightedly discovered in 1872. In Duns Scotus' vision and theology of the 'thisness' (*haecceitas*) of things, Hopkins found resonances with his own understanding of God's world, which has its own particular and unique identity, its inscape, reaching beyond particular species and objects into each one's individual expression. So, we do not know a rock by its basic qualities as a rock but through its own *individual* essence as a specific rock; we know a fish as an individual fish or a human being as an individual human being.

Like 'The Windhover', 'As Kingfishers Catch Fire' is a poem of Christ's presence; but here the effect is to scatter that presence widely, in all things, from a stone to a human life. This is the world pulsing with the incarnate Word, with life and purpose; all are expressed in language woven by the poet to flame into life in a moment of 'instress' within us, as we are invited to apprehend, to catch and glimpse, the inscape of another. There is something celebratory and intimate about being beckoned, by language, into an encounter with the God-given, Christ-dwelling inscape of other things in all their deepest, divine identity.

So it is that in 'As Kingfishers Catch Fire', we discover language that reaches into the heart of life, through alliterative turns, repetition and shifting stresses, taking us on a journey of sound and sight through God's kingdom. The poem begins as if we are glimpsing a bird caught in mid flight and, as is in the nature of a kingfisher – *this* kingfisher – it 'catch[es] fire' as it goes. Just 'as kingfishers catch fire', the poet says, so 'dragonflies draw flame'. It is their nature: flashing and hovering, shedding light in their iridescent yellows and reds, greens and goldens. More than this, while these creatures both, in their own way, fire and flash, so stones and bells both, in their own voices, chime and ring out their God-given identity – their inscape – into the world as they 'fling out' their 'broad name':

> As tumbled over rim in roundy wells
> Stones ring; like each tucked string tells, each hung bell's
> Bow swung finds tongue to fling out broad its name.

As we hover with kingfishers and dragonflies, and tumble and ring with stones and bells, we are taken into a landscape chattering with the voices of God's creation, each speaking itself into the world, declaring its own rich identity in the contours of its life. This, says Hopkins in 'As Kingfishers Catch Fire', is what we are called to – to be our deepest selves, as created by the Creator. 'Each mortal thing,' he goes on, stressing on the *one* thing to which we are called, which is the *same* for each of us:

> Deals out that being indoors each one dwells;
> Selves — goes itself; *myself* it speaks and spells,
> Crying Whát I dó is me: for that I came.

We cannot help, says Hopkins, but 'deal out' the self that lives within us; our very existence pours out into the world the self that God has called into being. The poetry itself speaks this out, with the striding sounds of Bs and Ds, with stresses and closely packed half-rhymes rolling from one line to the next ('dwells; / selves'). Language rolls and spills to express that – just as kingfishers catch fire, and dragonflies draw flame, and rocks and bells intone – we human creatures echo God's Word in speaking ourselves into the world, simply by existing. 'Whát I dó is me: for that I came'. We cannot but speak, as this is our purpose and our calling.

Hopkins moves, after the turn from octet to sestet, to 'say more' as we reach further into the calling of all things – all people – to live out their own *haecceitas*. The 'just man', he says, behaves in a way that befits his unique characteristics: 'the just man justices' (does justice). As the verse unfolds, we are shown reflections of becoming what we are called to be in language, which inverts and mirrors and amplifies so that the vantage point of seeing seems to change.

> I say móre: the just man justices;
>   Keeps grace: thát keeps all his goings graces;
> Acts in God's eye what in God's eye he is —
>   Chríst —;

There is grace and there is justice; but there is also a heart open to the claim laid up on each of us. It is no longer so much that we are shown the inscape of our fellow creatures and objects in God's world – from kingfisher to dragonflies and from stone to bell – but that we are shown ourselves from God's vantage point. Because the just, the graceful

> Acts in God's eye what in God's eye he is —
>   Chríst — for Christ plays in ten thousand places,
> Lovely in limbs, and lovely in eyes not his
>   To the Father through the features of men's faces.

All things – all people – are, to God, Christ. For Christ 'plays out in ten thousand places' and appears to God in 'eyes not his'. This is the life of Christ coursing through all things, all people, and visible to God. In these final heart-stopping lines, we discover that as we gaze on God's creatures and discover their unique Christ-ness, Christ, 'through the features of men's faces', gazes upon and is visible to his Father.

'As Kingfishers Catch Fire' offers a vision of God-with-us in the depths of our world and our being; it invites us to catch a glimpse of our unique, particular pattern, placed within us and called out of us. Perhaps, as we linger over this poem while we accompany Christ in the passionate, death-defying, life-defying Passion, we too might find that we are able to see ourselves through God's eyes: precious, beloved and carrying Christ through 'eyes not his' but our own.

Day 21

Friday

The Handsome Heart

'But tell me, child, your choice; what shall I buy
You?'—'Father, what you buy me I like best.'
With the sweetest air that said, still plied and pressed,
He swung to his first poised purport of reply.

What the heart is! which, like carriers let fly—
Doff darkness, homing nature knows the rest—
To its own fine function, wild and self-instressed,
Falls light as ten years long taught how to and why.

Mannerly-hearted! more than handsome face —
Beauty's bearing or muse of mounting vein,
All, in this case, bathed in high hallowing grace ...

Of heaven what boon to buy you, boy, or gain
Not granted?—Only ... O on that path you pace
Run all your race, O brace sterner that strain!

The condition of the human heart was of profound significance for Hopkins. In all its depths and distresses, the heart for him was neither a sentimental cypher nor a 'piece of flesh, the great bloodvessel only'; it was the home of thought and of the 'feelings of the soul to which it beats'.[60] To poetry rich with the subtleties of his own vagrant, faithful heart, Hopkins brought a profound understanding of the heart as the home and forge of the human character in relation to God, with its mercurial blend of seeking 'unteachably after evil' but also 'uttering truth'.[61]

From verse that grasps the heart's changes over time ('Spring and Fall') to the reserved, desiring heart of 'The Windhover', as well as to the wounded heart-soul, seeking loving kindness in 'My own heart let me more have pity on', the heart weaves through Hopkins' poetry – and finds a place in his sermons. In a sermon given one Sunday evening in November 1879, he preached of Christ's beauty: 'No heart as his was ever so tender, but tenderness was not all: this heart so tender was as brave. It could be stern.'[62]

'The Handsome Heart', written earlier that same year (and printed here from Robert Bridges' edition of Hopkins' poetry), offers a glimpse of Hopkins' textured relationship with the human heart. The poem described (as he shared in a letter to Bridges) an event during Lent the previous year when, without the help of a fellow clergyman, he was supported by two young members of the congregation. 'I offered them money for their services,' he wrote to Bridges. Both refused but when the elder boy then accepted, the younger, said Hopkins, 'followed suit; then when some days after I asked him what I shd. buy answered as in the sonnet;'[63] and this response became a source of wonder. Taking us straight into the midst of this moment, the poem begins:

'But tell me, child, your choice; what shall I buy
You?'

There is no precursor to explain what led up to it; but together with the following alliterative 'child' and 'choice', we quickly discover that *this* choice made by *this* child, stressed with gentle emphasis, will reveal much of the handsome heart that makes this choice. This emphasis reaches its height at the beginning of the second line with 'You', then 'gracefully falls away' (as Hopkins described in his letter to Bridges) into a 'diminuendo'. 'Little graces' such as these, said Hopkins to his friend, could help his verse to 'flow';[64] but perhaps strangely, it is in the dying fall of the boy's response that we find the heart and soul of the poem.

'Father, what you buy me I like best,' the boy says in the falling words that had so affected the poet. Pressed for an answer, this handsome heart, as if borne by flighted carriers that 'doff' – take off, remove – darkness, instinctively draws close to its own nature: its 'own fine function, wild and self-instressed', and shows its deepest instincts. This is a heart that reaches within to a natural depth of feeling, blending character and grace while surrendering need and desire to another. It is as if, in seeing the 'wild and self-instressed' response of the open-hearted boy, Hopkins himself instresses and receives in the depths of his own heart this momentary, contagious vision of the heart's beauty. And yet the dappled nature of the heart remains; there is the hint of a 'fall'. And whether this is the feather-light landing of an untrammelled heart or the prospect of a heavier fall, when the lightness of 'ten years long taught' has passed, is difficult to say. But for now, we are shown a heart that may discover itself in a deeply held potential for grace, beauty and character.

> What the heart is! which, like carriers let fly—
> Doff darkness, homing nature knows the rest—
> To its own fine function, wild and self-instressed,
> Falls light as ten years long taught how to and why.

In the turning of the sestet, we hear Hopkins' conviction that beauty is not to be found in form or favour, but 'bathed in high hallowing grace ... / Of heaven'. In this interweaving of divine and human, it seems that for Hopkins the depth of the heart – its deepest 'self-instress' – is in discovering itself within the love of God, as he reflected in spiritual notes written a year later.[65]

Here, he recorded the intensity of knowing ourselves and seeing the world through our own eyes and no one else's, with all our 'pleasures and pains ... deserts and guilt ... shame and sense of beauty, dangers, hopes, fears'. And yet, individual, rich, mixed and unique as we all are, 'human nature can have been developed, evolved ... not anyhow, ... but only by one of finer or higher pitch and determination than itself'.[66] The richness of our humanity – our character, our hearts – is ultimately rooted in God, said Hopkins; it is 'bathed in high hallowing grace ... / Of heaven'. 'May your heart remain true to the path you are on,' Hopkins appears to pray finally for this boy, who has shown him the heart's potential to show God's grace: 'on that path you pace / Run all your race'.

Motley, pure, wounded and yearning though the heart may be, in 'The Handsome Heart' Hopkins shows us an encounter with a heart seeming to beat in time with God's grace; he reveals the power of such a heart, the seat of character forged by gift and grace, to shape his own. May the dappled heart we open to Christ on our Lenten journey be open to the same transformative gift of grace.

Day 22

Saturday

The Habit of Perfection

Elected Silence, sing to me
And beat upon my whorlèd ear,
Pipe me to pastures still and be
The music that I care to hear.

Shape nothing, lips; be lovely-dumb:
It is the shut, the curfew sent
From there where all surrenders come
Which only makes you eloquent.

Be shellèd, eyes, with double dark
And find the uncreated light:
This ruck and reel which you remark
Coils, keeps, and teases simple sight.

Palate, the hutch of tasty lust,
Desire not to be rinsed with wine:
The can must be so sweet, the crust
So fresh that come in fasts divine!

Nostrils, your careless breath that spend
Upon the stir and keep of pride,
What relish shall the censers send
Along the sanctuary side!

O feel-of-primrose hands, O feet
That want the yield of plushy sward,
But you shall walk the golden street
And you unhouse and house the Lord.

And, Poverty, be thou the bride
And now the marriage feast begun,
And lily-coloured clothes provide
Your spouse not laboured-at nor spun.

On 23 January 1866, in the same month that he wrote 'The Habit of Perfection', the young Gerard Manley Hopkins looked ahead to the Lenten season and described his own privations: 'For Lent. No pudding on Sundays ... Ash Wednesday and Good Friday bread and water.'[67]

Not yet 22, Hopkins was still an undergraduate at Balliol College, in the middle of creative and charged years of discovery and learning: poetry and art; turbulent feelings and deeply formed friendships. Hopkins knew growing tensions as his richly creative, poetic soul and sensual engagement with the world blossomed alongside his intense spiritual life and his pull towards a religious vocation. The blending and battling of so variegated a character brought a lacerating, self-imposed austerity; the young poet was on continuous alert for his shortcomings, counting among them a deep sensitivity to beauty. All of this gave birth to an intensity of soul-searching, out of which emerged, in 1866, 'The Habit of Perfection', a hymn to the senses re-shaped as pathways of worship.

Often seen as one of Hopkins' most ascetic poems, 'The Habit of Perfection' seems to be more textured than this might suggest. We may discover in its language the sparseness of renunciation; but we may also glimpse something of his vivid engagement with the world and the depth of spiritual yearning. The poem begins and ends with singing silence and rich poverty; it draws us into the tensions and riches of a life surrendered to God. The regular, structured four-line verses (each with four stresses), give the poem a hymn-like regularity. But there is also a soundscape and alliterative flourishes that bring an inviting verve to this disciplined shape – so that we might also yearn for that same silence as Hopkins, that same dark seeing, that same savour and scent, and that same touch of heaven and earth.

The poem begins with a mesmerizing call to silence, expressed in gentle sibilants. It is as if silence is a separate entity, even though it has been chosen:

> Elected Silence, sing to me
> And beat upon my whorlèd ear,
> Pipe me to pastures still and be
> The music that I care to hear.

This is a silence with a music of its own: singing, 'beating' on the rounded contours of the poet's 'whorlèd' ear and 'piping' him – leading him towards a destination – as if piped aboard a ship, with a frequency of sound that rises above the shriek of the waves. Here, he is led away from life's clamour and led to 'pastures still'. Finally, the call is for this silent music to be resolved into a musical silence, which may be a place of surrender and encounter.

As the poet turns towards speech fallen silent, the surrender deepens. 'Shape nothing, lips; be lovely-dumb'. Do not speak, we hear: there is beauty in silence. And it may only be when we are called to silence by a 'curfew' that true surrender comes; and from there, *true* eloquence may emerge. This may be our own eloquence; but perhaps God, the one who calls us to surrender, is made eloquent as we fall silent.

Vision, taste and scent are also brought before us in a vivid re-shaping of senses, calling us to discover through and beyond them the Giver of all life. 'Be shellèd, eyes, with double dark', says Hopkins, bidding his own eyes to be closed and covered ('shellèd'), and so 'find the uncreated light' that emanates from God's presence. And in language that offers a glimpse of the poetic richness to come, he counterpoints this inner vision with the alliterative bounce of the 'ruck and reel', on which we usually focus our gaze, and that 'coils, keeps, and teases' us, grabbing our attention and derailing our 'simple sight'. Taste, too, is to be re-directed. He asks his palate, the 'hutch' or home of 'tasty lust', to turn away from taste for its own sake and towards the savour of God tasted in 'fasts divine'; this is both fast and feast, as 'wine' and 'crust' (with their echoes of the Eucharist) transform taste for worship.

Perhaps the most curious verse is that dedicated to scent. Here, we find no ordinary juxtaposition of a beautiful, tempting scent against one redolent of God's presence but, instead, a juxtaposition of pride and humility.

> Nostrils, your careless breath that spend
> Upon the stir and keep of pride,
> What relish shall the censers send
> Along the sanctuary side!

We might hear in these lines a simple breath spent on all the commotion ('stir') of life; or we might hear a snort of derision, of one caught in 'keep[ing]' their own pride; or, perhaps, imprisoned in the 'keep' of their own pride. This self-focused breath becomes transformed into a fragrance that turns us towards God, in the all-enveloping fragrance of incense, all 'along the sanctuary side'. Here is a place of worship or safety; perhaps this is also where Hopkins, with a hovering sense of calling to the Church, hopes to have his very breath shaped by and towards God, who fills us with his spirit. And as Hopkins turns towards touch, this hovering sense of call lingers. He conjures before us the 'feel-of-primrose' touch of hands on gossamer soft flowers and feet that lack or desire ('want') the feel of grass. These same feet, Hopkins reflects, will 'walk the golden street': perhaps in heaven or perhaps in an earthly life made golden by fulfilling a sense of call, in which he might 'unhouse and house the Lord', called upon by others to consecrate bread ('unhous[ing] the Lord), while also 'hous[ing]' God as a bearer of God's light and presence in a life consecrated to service.

In the final verse, the sense of calling draws closer. From the silence at the beginning of 'The Habit of Perfection', we have been drawn through the 'uncreated light' of God, the savour, scent and touch of God's life, and brought finally to a deep recognition of the richness of surrender. In addressing 'Poverty', Hopkins brings before himself (and us) the choice to live simply; more than this, he hints at that poverty of spirit which draws us into surrender and reliance on God the Giver of all gifts and source of all life. Now it is time to be clothed in 'lily-coloured' robes, with all the echoes of the Gospel of Matthew's 'lilies of the field',[68] glorious in their naturally nurtured life. 'Lily-coloured clothes' provided by poverty are 'not laboured-at nor spun', but freely given and naturally worn:

And, Poverty, be thou the bride
And now the marriage feast begun,
And lily-coloured clothes provide
Your spouse not laboured-at nor spun.

'The Habit of Perfection' carries the traces of that wrestling, vivid inner life and embryonic calling that shaped the young Gerard Manley Hopkins' life in Oxford. If we find a certain innocence and zeal in his passion, we may also find riches in his exploration of senses called into service for God. Whether we read the poem as one of renunciation, transformation or a blend of both, we may find that we are left with our own questions. We may ask ourselves whether – and how – we experience God in the depths of our senses, and whether we bring our senses before God. We may also ask ourselves how we might know and surrender to our Saviour as we meet him in singing silence and rich poverty on the journey through Lent.

Day 23

Monday

Justus Quidem (Thou art indeed just, Lord)

Justus quidem tu es, Domine, si disputem tecum;
  verumtamen
justa loquar ad te: quare via impiorum prosperatur?
  (from Jeremiah 12:1)

Thou art indeed just, Lord, if I contend
With thee; but, sir, so what I plead is just.
Why do sinners' ways prosper? and why must
Disappointment all I endeavour end?

Wert thou my enemy, O thou my friend,
How wouldst thou worse, I wonder, than thou dost
Defeat, thwart me? Oh, the sots and thralls of lust
Do in spare hours more thrive than I that spend,

Sir, life upon thy cause. See, banks and brakes
Now, leavèd how thick! lacèd they are again
With fretty chervil, look, and fresh wind shakes

Them; birds build — but not I build; no, but strain,
Time's eunuch, and not breed one work that wakes.
Mine, O thou lord of life, send my roots rain.

At the beginning of 1889, Hopkins was on retreat in Tullabeg, in the middle of Ireland. His retreat notes of this time tell us much of his mind and heart early in this final year of his life. In them, he poured out his heart about his five-year struggle to feel at home in Ireland and his reflections on his priestly calling.

He had, he wrote, remained sure of his calling to his chosen

JUSTUS QUIDEM (THOU ART INDEED JUST, LORD)

church home but was unsure of his 'outward' living of his calling and was 'ashamed of the little I have done, of my waste of time'.[69] Also troubled by the travails and actions of his Church at this time, he laboured through a feeling of being compromised and drawn into a cause not of his choosing.[70] Describing his dappled sense of vocation – at once sure in its overall pattern and texture, and lacking in confidence and conviction in its more finely grained weave – Hopkins mused in his retreat notes on 'the anticipation of happiness hereafter ... but it is not happiness now'. 'What is life without aim, without spur, without help?' he asked. 'All my undertakings miscarry: I am like a straining eunuch.'[71]

Depleted, too, by tiredness and low spirits, Hopkins wrote that he could 'do no more than repeat, *Justus es, Domine, et rectum judicium tuum*': 'You are righteous, O LORD, and your judgements are right,' from the opening of Jeremiah 12. Just a few weeks later, this voice emerged in his poem 'Justus Quidem'. It was on St Patrick's Day in 1889, the second Sunday of Lent that year, that Hopkins sat down to write this sonnet, with its blend of prayer and supplication, lament and wrestling with the God who calls – and a plea for the new life that follows our Lenten journey. Here was the voice of Hopkins as priest, drawing on readings from the Lenten mass of the time,[72] and as skilled poet, yearning for inspiration. There is also a hint of the prophet in Hopkins (wrestling like Jeremiah in 'exile' from home), inspired to create this poem of simplicity and complexity. While 'Justus Quidem' begins close in spirit and meaning to the opening of Jeremiah 12, it gradually takes us further away in theme, tone and language, deftly knitting together Scripture and the journey of *this* human soul.

The first three lines present us with a clear echo of Jeremiah, with a paradoxical desire to declare a just God and to voice a sense of injustice. Hopkins begins with

> Thou art indeed just, Lord, if I contend
> With thee; but, sir, so what I plead is just.
> Why do sinners' ways prosper?

DAY 23: MONDAY

In Jeremiah 12, we hear:

> You will be in the right, O Lord,
>   when I lay charges against you;
>   but let me put my case to you.
> Why does the way of the guilty prosper?
>   Why do all who are treacherous thrive?

Here are adoration and challenge, devotion and frustration in a prayer-poem, echoing the very human desire both to worship and to question God (who loves all equally), when, in our hearts, we want to be favoured over the 'sinners' and the 'guilty' who prosper. How, both poet and prophet ask, can the prosperity of the wicked be justified? At this point, poem and Scripture begin to diverge in the first of two distinct shifts that take Hopkins' poem in a different direction.

Jeremiah continues to struggle in general terms with the prosperity of the wicked. But in 'Justus Quidem', a startlingly new and direct voice emerges: it is as if Hopkins is losing himself in the Scripture, discovering its meaning for him, and expressing the pain of feeling singled out for suffering. 'Why must / Disappointment all I endeavour end?' he asks. And, confused by his paradoxical experiences of injustice with a just God, he appeals personally to God, his friend, to ask what worse could happen to him, if God were his enemy.

> Wert thou my enemy, O thou my friend,
> How wouldst thou worse, I wonder, than thou dost
> Defeat, thwart me? Oh, the sots and thralls of lust
> Do in spare hours more thrive than I that spend,
>
> Sir, life upon thy cause.

This new voice takes us into the heart of Hopkins' religious experience – and may touch our own. We hear the deep lament, the love and rage, which can shape our prayer at times of confused adoration and which, faith tells us, can be hurled,

JUSTUS QUIDEM (THOU ART INDEED JUST, LORD)

without rejection, at God, whose justice we demand and whose love overwhelms us. The first half line of the sestet, 'Sir, life upon thy cause,' sharpens the sting of Hopkins' lament, as these words could suggest genuine or mock respect – or even a rebuke of God; but then the poem shifts again, as if the sharpness of his words open a flood of muse-beckoned images. Writing only weeks after lamenting his poetic wasteland and that 'all [his] undertakings miscarry', Hopkins' conjures a natural world overflowing with a creativity to which he does not feel equal, but in language that clearly shows his creative power:

> See, banks and brakes
> Now, leavèd how thick! lacèd they are again
> With fretty chervil, look, and fresh wind shakes
>
> Them; birds build — but not I build; no, but strain,
> Time's eunuch, and not breed one work that wakes.
> Mine, O thou lord of life, send my roots rain.

Hopkins may see himself as 'time's eunuch' – unable to bring his poetry to birth, to 'breed one work that wakes' – but his lament is so richly crafted in its bounding rhythm and inverting, echoing sounds that it somehow speaks movement ('fretty chervil, look, and fresh wind shakes') into the landscape. If this hints at (or expresses) a kind of awakening embedded in the very heart of the poem, the last line takes it further in a prayer: 'Mine, O thou lord of life, send my roots rain.' The tone here is softer and the plea becomes more heartfelt and personal in the echoing of 'mine' and 'my'. 'Send my roots rain', pleads the poet, in a heart-opening prayer for new life to break into his personal wasteland.

If 'Justus Quidem' is a mirror for our own puzzled questions, it may also be an invitation to reach into and through our faithful struggle, and to seek the waters that will bring life to our Lenten wilderness, in all its rigour and richness.

> Mine, O thou lord of life, send my roots rain.

Day 24

Tuesday

The Leaden Echo

(Maidens' song from St Winefred's Well)

How to keep—is there ány any, is there none such, nowhere known some, bow or brooch or braid or brace, láce, latch or catch or key to keep
Back beauty, keep it, beauty, beauty, beauty, ... from vanishing away?
Ó is there no frowning of these wrinkles, rankèd wrinkles deep,
Dówn? no waving off of these most mournful messengers, still messengers, sad and stealing messengers of grey?
No there's none, there's none, O no there's none,
Nor can you long be, what you now are, called fair,
Do what you may do, what, do what you may,
And wisdom is early to despair:
Be beginning; since, no, nothing can be done
To keep at bay
Age and age's evils, hoar hair,
Ruck and wrinkle, drooping, dying, death's worst, winding sheets, tombs and worms and tumbling to decay;
So be beginning, be beginning to despair.
O there's none; no no no there's none:
Be beginning to despair, to despair,
Despair, despair, despair, despair.

Just a few miles from St Beuno's is the small village of Holywell, the site of the ancient St Winefred's Well. A destination of Christian pilgrimage since the seventh century, this was a resonant place for Hopkins, close as it was to his heart's home and filled with the mystery of ancient landscapes, sainthood and sacredness. Among its saints was St Winefred, whose story became the inspiration of a composition that was years in the writing but never completed.

According to legend, Holywell (or Treffynon) in Flintshire is the site of the martyrdom of St Winefred, a Welsh saint of the seventh century. The different versions of the legend, surviving in different manuscripts, tell us that Winefred, the daughter of a local landowner and the niece of St Beuno himself, was an early follower of this saint who had decided to build a monastic house in the area. Committing her life to God, she repulsed the advances of the local prince Caradoc. In a rage, he took her head from her body. St Beuno – who, according to legend, was saying mass at the time, passing by or retrieving Winefred's head from where it had rolled (and where the well later emerged) – is said to have restored her to life. Caradoc, on the other hand, was consigned to death, swallowed up in the landscape. Legend also tells us that Winefred later became an abbess, that she lived a long life of devotion to God, and that her body was finally taken to Shrewsbury Abbey.

This drama of sacred commitment inspired Hopkins' verse-version, begun in 1880. Though he never finished the whole work, he completed part of it, which is known as 'The Leaden Echo and the Golden Echo' in 1882. It is shot through with the inscape of a soul's surrender of what we most cling to: the beauty of youth, which is the fantasy of immortality.

'The Leaden Echo', our focus for today, pulses with the chant of the maidens of the Holy Well and the sadness of surrendering that fantasy of immortality. For all its pining pain, there is also an intoxicating movement in the poem, which 'carr[ies] the reader along'.[73] We, too, can be carried along, hearing the force of the poem's message through the insistent chant of chiming, echoing words, which transforms a not-uncommon spiritual theme into a vivid picture of faithful experience.

The opening lines establish the verbal echoes that will suffuse the language. 'How to keep,' the poem asks straight away; but only in line 4 do we understand the question, which is 'How to keep ... / Back beauty?' In the intervening lines, sounds repeat and rhyme and echo through shifting words to open up the meaning when it comes. 'How are we to keep back beauty from vanishing away?' asks Hopkins. Is there any way? 'Any,' says the unstressed echo of the maidens. Their questioning plea continues; and we find ourselves following the desire to unlock *any* clue to holding on to beauty, on to human immortality, as words change sound by sound, drawing us on. 'Bow' moves to 'brooch' and to 'braid'; 'lace' to 'latch' to 'catch' to 'key' – and back to 'keep' – and so we are swept back to the question: 'How to keep back beauty?' 'Keep it,' we hear, 'beauty, beauty, beauty,' echoing our yearning, shape-shifting emotional world as we resist life's changes:

> How to keep—is there ány any, is there none such, nowhere known some, bow or brooch or braid or brace, láce, latch or catch or key to keep
> Back beauty, keep it, beauty, beauty, beauty, ... from vanishing away?

The questioning goes on, asking if there is a way of being rid of the 'mournful messengers' – wrinkles and greyness – that tell the story of life's passing. The answer, when it comes, is 'No there's none, there's none, O no there's none.' Nothing can be done to 'keep at bay / Age and age's evils'. In sounds that seem to bounce off wilderness rocks, laments pour out; and we may be left wondering whether we are hearing some angelic call for release from the scourge of mortal beauty or an echo of the maidens' inner turmoil thrown outwards, lamenting the loss of loveliness in life's passing. This is a wilderness-testing of desire and surrender; but there may also be a spark of wisdom.

'Be beginning,' we have heard and will hear again. And in a passage that gradually picks up speed as words change and draw us on in their skin-sloughing transformations, we are taken on a journey to life's end:

THE LEADEN ECHO

> Ruck and wrinkle, drooping, dying, death's worst, winding
> sheets, tombs and worms and tumbling to decay.

So, sing the maidens, 'be beginning, be beginning to despair', because

> O there's none; no no no there's none:
> Be beginning to despair, to despair,
> Despair, despair, despair, despair.

It is here that we may catch a glimpse of wisdom – in a dim and stumbling recognition of life's limits – as we see that beauty, human immortality, is not ours to grasp.

It may be that, in 'The Leaden Echo', we hear the footfall of life's passing and the quietly chanting voices that announce our own mortality. We may also find ourselves asking Lenten questions about what we are tempted to 'keep back', beauty or otherwise, and what we hoard in our own wilderness-testing of desire and surrender. We have time to reflect on this. The ending of 'The Leaden Echo' is not the final word; tomorrow, in 'The Golden Echo', we pick up on the echo of an echo.

Day 25

Wednesday

The Golden Echo

(Maidens' song from St Winefred's Well)

                      Spare!
There is one, yes I have one (Hush there!);
Only not within seeing of the sun,
Not within the singeing of the strong sun,
Tall sun's tingeing, or treacherous the tainting of the earth's air.
Somewhere elsewhere there is ah well where! one,
Óne. Yes I can tell such a key, I do know such a place,
Where whatever's prized and passes of us, everything that's fresh and fast flying of us, seems to us sweet of us and swiftly away with, done away with, undone,
Undone, done with, soon done with, and yet dearly and dangerously sweet
Of us, the wimpled-water-dimpled, not-by-morning-matchèd face,
The flower of beauty, fleece of beauty, too too apt to, ah! to fleet,
Never fleets more, fastened with the tenderest truth
To its own best being and its loveliness of youth: it is an everlastingness of, O it is an all youth!
Come then, your ways and airs and looks, locks, maiden gear, gallantry and gaiety and grace,
Winning ways, airs innocent, maiden manners, sweet looks, loose locks, long locks, lovelocks, gaygear, going gallant, girlgrace—

Resign them, sign them, seal them, send them, motion them
   with breath,
And with sighs soaring, soaring síghs deliver
Them; beauty-in-the-ghost, deliver it, early now, long
   before death
Give beauty back, beauty, beauty, beauty, back to God,
   beauty's self and beauty's giver.
See; not a hair is, not an eyelash, not the least lash lost;
   every hair
Is, hair of the head, numbered.
Nay, what we had lighthanded left in surly the mere mould
Will have waked and have waxed and have walked with the
   wind what while we slept,
This side, that side hurling a heavyheaded hundredfold
What while we, while we slumbered.
O then, weary then whý should we tread? O why are we
   so haggard at the heart, so care-coiled, care-killed, so
   fagged, so fashed, so cogged, so cumbered,
When the thing we freely fórfeit is kept with fonder a care,
Fonder a care kept than we could have kept it, kept
Far with fonder a care (and we, we should have lost it)
   finer, fonder
A care kept. Where kept? Do but tell us where kept, where.—
Yonder.—What high as that! We follow, now we follow.—
   Yonder, yes yonder, yonder,
Yonder.

The ending of 'The Leaden Echo' is not the final word. The question that it asked at its very beginning, and pursued as a haunting, plangent symphony of mortality, reaches towards a new understanding in 'The Golden Echo'. Yesterday's

> is there ány any, is there none such, nowhere known
>   some, bow or brooch or braid or brace, láce, latch or
>   catch or key to keep
> Back beauty, keep it, beauty, beauty, beauty, … from
>   vanishing away?

is met in today's opening:

> Spare!
> There is one, yes I have one (Hush there!);

We are immediately in a different landscape. 'Spare!' with its overtones of safety, of 'being spared', of forbearance – and with its rhyming echo of 'despair' (at the end of 'The Leaden Echo') – tilts the tone towards redemption. 'Spare': there is one way, one key to being released from the despair of our losses and life's passing; 'hush there,' we hear, take comfort. And from here, we are drawn into a dancing, shifting exploration: not of beauty, which fades as we cling to our mortality (the 'Ruck and wrinkle, drooping, dying, death's worst, winding sheets' of 'The Leaden Echo'), but of beauty surrendered to the one who has brought it to birth; beauty surrendered to the Creator of all beauty.

There is one 'key' to our release but it is 'not within seeing of the sun'; not within reach in our earthly life; 'not within the singeing of the strong sun'. This is in a place far from the 'treacherous ... tainting of the earth's air', where human beauty is both utterly present and completely ephemeral. It is 'prized and passes'; 'fresh and fast flying ... sweet of us and swiftly away with'; 'soon done with, and yet dearly and dangerously sweet / Of us'. Neither a place of decay nor of eternal earthly life and beauty, this one place holds both the freshness of the 'wimpled-water-dimpled ... face' and its passing: here is 'an everlastingness ... / ... an all youth!'

The poignancy of this – of beauty and its passing – is all expressed in language that leaps and dances, shifts and doubles back, rhyming and echoing; language inspired by the 'consonant-chime' (*cynghanedd*) of Welsh poetry, which so appealed to Hopkins' technical scrupulosity and to his word-breaking style, breathing life into the words themselves. He felt he 'never did anything more musical' than this poem,[74] with its vibrant, questioning and echoing soundscape: one that unfolds throughout 'The Golden Echo', as it explores the one

THE GOLDEN ECHO

place, the one way of keeping the glories of earthly beauty – with its 'airs and looks, locks, maiden gear, gallantry and gaiety and grace' – and that is to surrender them. 'Resign them, sign them, seal them, send them, motion them with breath,' says the poet, with insistent sibilant stresses and repetitions.

> And with sighs soaring, soaring síghs deliver
> Them; beauty-in-the-ghost, deliver it, early now, long
>   before death
> Give beauty back, beauty, beauty, beauty, back to God,
>   beauty's self and beauty's giver.

This is a kind of surrender that feels physical, as if it is through an exhaled release that it takes place, with 'breath' and 'sighs soaring, soaring sighs deliver/ Them'; and then 'beauty-in-the-ghost' shimmers, with a sense of beauty within, with the Spirit of God and perhaps with a 'shade' or shadow of beauty. Beauty, we are told, must be 'given back' to its giver. And what might seem an expression of asceticism emerges as a profound understanding of our mortality, kept deeply within the heart of God, where nothing is lost. 'See,' the poet goes on,

>   not a hair is, not an eyelash, not the least lash lost;
>   every hair
> Is, hair of the head, numbered.

This surrender is not an abandonment of our humanity, but a deep recognition of where our humanity is most beloved, most protected. So the question arises in 'The Golden Echo', asked by the maidens: why do we do we exhaust ourselves in the battle of life when surrender is a release? 'Weary then whý should we tread? O why are we so haggard at the / heart, so care-coiled, care-killed, so fagged, so fashed' when, in surrendering what we 'freely fórfeit', it is kept safely:

>   kept with fonder a care,
> Fonder a care kept than we could have kept it, kept

DAY 25 WEDNESDAY

> Far with fonder a care (and we, we should have lost it)
>   finer, fonder
> A care kept.

A care kept. By the end of 'The Golden Echo', we find ourselves circling back to the beginning of 'The Leaden Echo'. 'How to keep ... / Back beauty ... from vanishing / away,' we began yesterday; now we hear that this 'keeping' is not within our gift but in the gift of the One who keeps all things.

Together, these two parts – 'The Leaden Echo' and 'The Golden Echo' – guide us towards a vision of life enhanced, transfigured by the act of surrender. We can do nothing to preserve ourselves from the insistent tread of earthly life, its ordinary wrinkles and its ravages on the way to its inevitable end. To know that this is so, and to surrender our morality to the Giver of life and beauty, is to be freed from investing in an impossible dream of stopping time and 'holding back' beauty; to embrace instead the boundless grace of eternity in which all 'is kept with fonder a care ... / ... than we could have kept it'.

The challenge is clear (and it is a deeply Lenten challenge), with questions about what we cling to and what we surrender; about what we seek to control and what we cede to God; about what holds us in the wilderness and what fills us with life. These are questions about following and allowing ourselves to be led into the eternity in which all things are kept.

>   Where kept? Do but tell us where kept, where.—
> Yonder.—What high as that! We follow, now we follow.—
>   Yonder, yes yonder, yonder,
> Yonder.

Day 26

Thursday

Thee, God, I come from, to thee go

Thee, God, I come from, to thee go,
All day long I like fountain flow
From thy hand out, swayed about
Mote-like in thy mighty glow.

What I know of thee I bless,
As acknowledging thy stress
On my being and as seeing
Something of thy holiness.

Once I turned from thee and hid,
Bound on what thou hadst forbid;
Sow the wind I would; I sinned:
I repent of what I did.

Bad I am, but yet thy child.
Father, be thou reconciled
Spare thou me, since I see
With thy might that thou art mild.

I have life before me still
And thy purpose to fulfil;
Yea a debt to pay thee yet:
Help me, sir, and so I will.

DAY 26: THURSDAY

> But thou bidst, and just thou art,
> Me shew mercy from my heart
> Towards my brother, every other
> Man my mate and counterpart.

When, in 1893, Hopkins' friend Robert Bridges had the opportunity to include some of his late friend's poems in an anthology, one of eight he chose was 'Thee, God, I come from'.[75] In a body of work which is now known more for its harlequin-flourishes, intensity and spiritual insight into the natural world, it is perhaps surprising that this gentle, devotional and apparently simple poem should stand as an early landmark of Hopkins' poetic gift and originality.

Probably written towards the end of 1885, the poem has a poignant stillness that follows the poetic storms of his sequence of 'Terrible Sonnets'. Here, we find little of the 'natural eccentricity' and 'extravagance' that his friend Bridges saw in Hopkins' mature poetic style.[76] There is, instead, the hum of a regular rhythm, leavened by an unusual rhyme scheme (aab / ba): a rhythm that invests the whole with gentle movement and takes us through repeated, prayerful recognitions of the grace of God, unnamed in the poem but suffusing it with his presence.

A little like the swooping returns of 'The Windhover', this is a poem of circular movement; of breathing out towards God, who fills us in the return with the breath of his Spirit, and then out again, to the next of its six short verses. In each, we join the poet-narrator's reflection on his relationship with God; and after an unusual and almost conversational centre to each verse (which adds a fluttering urgency as of a heart quickened in yearning prayer), we find ourselves in a moment of surrender, carried through a prayerful journey of discerning and discovering the heart's direction.

'Thee, God, I come from, to thee go,' the poem begins and immediately we are invited into the movement of breath and return that each short verse allows us to experience. The opening lines draw us into the gently expressed drama of faithful longing and belonging, of desire and worship, of self-giving, and of being drawn more deeply into the blend of human soul-searching and the claim of God in our lives. After the first line, we are taken into a fountain-flow of gift and grace, in which the poet, and we, seem to be a speck of dust ('mote-like') in the pouring force that emerges from God:

> Thee, God, I come from, to thee go,
> All day long I like fountain flow
> From thy hand out, swayed about
> Mote-like in thy mighty glow.

'Mote-like': there is a certain humility in this multivalent image that may conjure for us specks of dust glistening in a shaft of light streaming through a window. Or it may bring before us the 'motes and beams' that remind us of our dappled existence and our capacity to hide from our own shortcomings; our capacity to be drawn away from God. These are rich, simple words; but they have the power to bring us to a recognition both of our limitations – the dust of our being – and of the lustre we are given as we dance in the 'mighty glow' of God's presence.

The perspective shifts towards the second stanza and in all those that follow. We are taken onwards through a sequence of faith and feeling, adoration and sorrowful repentance: a prodigal-plea for reconciliation with God and recognition of grace and of God's claim on our lives. Finally, we are shown a heart turned outwards to others: all in deft language that somehow bears both the weight of God's glory and the vagaries and vacillations of the most faithful of hearts. The second verse, for example, opens with the poet's praise of God and immediately turns to the impact – the 'stress' – of God within him, crafting and shaping the heart that sees God's 'holiness':

> What I know of thee I bless,
> As acknowledging thy stress
> On my being and as seeing
> Something of thy holiness.

DAY 26: THURSDAY

And as in all the verses, the third line carries an inner rhyme that both halts us for a heartbeat and carries us on towards a final line, closing the thought of the stanza:

> thy stress
> On my *being* and as *seeing*
> Something.

The double rhyme in the third stanza is particularly poignant. In this verse, we move from 'Once I turned from thee and hid,' towards the final, resolving line, 'I repent of what I did,' by way of the heartfelt cry: 'Sow the wind I would; I sinned.' With an echo of Hosea (8.7), we hear the cry of one who is grasping the consequences of choices that can take us away, bit by bit, from God's presence. Through a breathing in and out of prayer and supplication, through thoughts that pivot and turn towards new realizations, and through a more deeply expressed sense of God's justice and mercy, the poem moves us towards the final verses: towards the poet-prayer's deep acknowledgement of God's claim on the whole of his life. Perhaps there is also an echo of the struggle to offer all that we have to God, with all the costliness of faith:

> I have life before me still
> And thy purpose to fulfil;
> Yea a debt to pay thee yet:
> Help me, sir, and so I will.
>
> But thou bidst, and just thou art,
> Me shew mercy from my heart
> Towards my brother, every other
> Man my mate and counterpart.

God requires, 'and just thou art', we hear, as if there is still the need to express the costliness of self-offering to the God from whom the poet-prayer comes and to whom he returns.

THEE, GOD, I COME FROM, TO THEE GO

'Thee, God, I come from' – with its gently expressed drama of faithful longing and belonging, desire, worship and surrender – may be for us a mirror of our own spiritual journey. To linger over its repeated in-breath and out-breath may be to draw closer to God and, in the middle of life's dappled chances and changes, to acknowledge and give thanks for the mystery of God with us through a journey of worship and repentance; and through seeking forgiveness, to discovering purpose and accepting God's claim on our lives. Finally, through the vision of the last verse, we may catch a glimpse of the deep desire within our mottled hearts to seek the grace to pour ourselves outwards towards God's creatures.

Day 27

Friday

Spring and Fall

to a young child

Márgarét, áre you gríeving
Over Goldengrove unleaving?
Leáves líke the things of man, you
With your fresh thoughts care for, can you?
Ah! ás the heart grows older
It will come to such sights colder
By and by, nor spare a sigh
Though worlds of wanwood leafmeal lie;
And yet you will weep and know why.
Now no matter, child, the name:
Sórrow's spríngs áre the same.
Nor mouth had, no nor mind, expressed
What heart heard of, ghost guessed:
It ís the blight man was born for,
It is Margaret you mourn for.

'Spring and Fall' begins with a bounce. This poem 'to a young child', with an apparent simplicity in its first two lines, seems to suggest that we are about to enter a gentle poetic world, expressed in a way that 'Margaret' can grasp. But there are clues from the outset that hint at a richer and more variegated landscape than we might expect.

'Margaret', the poem opens; and we might naturally have stressed – lingered over – certain syllables, in tune with a gently rhythmic poetic opening: 'Márgaret, áre you gríeving'. Instead, we are guided by the poet into a more insistent, more questioning tone, which immediately shifts the sense:

Márgarét, áre you gríeving
Over Goldengrove unleaving?

'Márgaret, áre you gríeving', we now hear. And a question that might seem simple takes on new shades and deepens to a plaintive enquiry; to a puzzled wonder ('*Are* you *grie*ving?'). From here, the tone of the whole poem opens up and looks ahead to a rich blend of experience, of feeling and of reflection. It has the potential to reach into our hearts and invite us to enter a liminal landscape of innocence and loss, of experience and knowing.

This sense of liminality might express something of Hopkins' season of life as he wrote 'Spring and Fall'. The poem was composed in Liverpool in early September 1880; it was three years since Hopkins had moved away from his beloved St Beuno's, where God had shone as from 'shook foil' and coloured his life as his own 'Goldengrove'. In the intervening time, his frequent moves had taught him the brutalizing bleakness of the industrial landscape and had brought him into the dark presence of deep poverty. And yet he felt 'born to deal with' parishioners caught in life's deepest daily struggles, as he said of the people of Bedford Leigh.[77]

The most searing move lay ahead of him; but it is as if, for now, we find Hopkins sitting in a liminal space between past joy and future distress – with the shimmering immediacy of God less accessible than in former days – and lost in the dappled reality of a different life, in different places. 'I remember that crimson and pure blues seemed to me spiritual and heavenly sights fit to draw tears once,' he wrote in a letter the same year. 'Now I can just see what I once saw, but can hardly dwell on it and should not care to do so.'[78]

'Spring and Fall' seems to reflect this loss of bright innocence. It hovers in this world and between worlds in a dancing, irregular pattern of Hopkins' sprung rhythm, inspired by the cadences of earlier English poetry and vernacular speech to create a more natural form of expression than the regular rhythms of the poetic register.[79] In sprung rhythm, the meaning of the poem is forged in sound as much as word, just as in ordinary speech meaning may be teased out, or layered, when we repeat, run stresses together, echo, double back and allow sound to rise or fall.

In 'Spring and Fall', we hear of Margaret's grieving, leaving and 'unleaving', with all the shifting and shimmering meaning of this word. It might bring to mind the 'unleaving' of autumn as leaves fall from newly 'unleaved' trees. Or we might think of the fall of humanity or our inevitable loss of innocence as childhood is left behind. And as the verse unfolds, it seems that we are caught in a dance between leaving, staying and re-understanding our 'unleaving' of Goldengrove. As life goes on, Hopkins seems to suggest, Margaret – and all of us – may find that our first 'fresh thoughts' will vanish as warm innocence gives way to a chillier experience of the world.

> Ah! ás the heart grows older
> It will come to such sights colder
> By and by, nor spare a sigh
> Though worlds of wanwood leafmeal lie.

Of course, with age, our hearts lose their passion and untrammelled innocence, suggests the poet, with his emphatic 'Ah!' and the stress on 'ás'. And with the words 'by and by' running gently on to another line, we are invited into the natural flow of time that seems to cool the warmth of life's Maytime. We become, it seems, gradually inured to the 'unleaving' of our world; we no longer sigh over the wintering of life or over the scattered fall of spring's growth through life's natural decay. This, it seems, is our lot.

Then the tone of the poem seems to shift. We find ourselves moving from loss of innocence to a rich blend of the natural chances and changes of life, and the wisdom of understanding our humanity as God's creatures. As she grows in wisdom and consciousness, Margaret will 'weep and know why'; she will know in her heart 'the blight man was born for':

> Nor mouth had, no nor mind, expressed
> What heart heard of, ghost guessed:
> It ís the blight man was born for,
> It is Margaret you mourn for.

With echoes of 1 Corinthians 2, in which we hear of the Spirit of God revealing to us 'what no eye has seen, nor ear heard, nor the human heart conceived' (v. 9), Hopkins invites us into the 'ghost guessed' intuitive understanding of mottled human nature. There seems to be a certain wisdom, we hear, at the heart of our sadness. Even in our innocent knowing, we have intimations of our blended nature, our 'blight' and propensity to be bent out of shape in a dappled, fallen world.

Suddenly, we are no longer solely in the loss and decay of passing youth; instead, we are in a layered and contoured world of innocence giving way to the wisdom and understanding that is gifted to us through the spirit of God, even in a fallen world. Perhaps finally, Margaret mourns herself and the ending of an innocence that must end; and perhaps it is our lot to mourn our own loss of innocence, which is the cost of self-knowing in our dappled humanity.

In the season of Lent, we are gifted again with the opportunity to enter a landscape of innocence and loss, of experience and knowing lived out in graced, fallen lives. This is a liminal space of losing and finding, in which, like Margaret, we are invited to explore who we are and who we are becoming. We are encouraged, too, to bring the whole of ourselves to the one who enters the wilderness on our behalf, facing self and God, while learning the losses and costs of a life that remains, gloriously, caught up in the grace and wisdom of God.

Day 28

Saturday

Binsey Poplars Felled 1879

    My aspens dear, whose airy cages quelled,
    Quelled or quenched in leaves the leaping sun,
    All felled, felled, are all felled;
      Of a fresh and following folded rank
          Not spared, not one
          That dandled a sandalled
        Shadow that swam or sank
On meadow & river & wind-wandering weed-winding bank.

    O if we but knew what we do
        When we delve or hew —
      Hack and rack the growing green!
        Since country is so tender
    To touch, her being só slender,
    That, like this sleek and seeing ball
    But a prick will make no eye at all,
    Where we, even where we mean
          To mend her we end her,
        When we hew or delve:
After-comers cannot guess the beauty been.
      Ten or twelve, only ten or twelve
        Strokes of havoc unselve
          The sweet especial scene,
    Rural scene, a rural scene,
    Sweet especial rural scene.

BINSEY POPLARS

Just a couple of miles to the west of Balliol College in Oxford lies the village of Binsey. Binsey and nearby Godstow had been favourite destinations for Hopkins as a student, often visited by road or river, with friends or alone. And 12 years after graduating, he returned.

Already with several moves behind him, Hopkins came back to Oxford to serve as a curate at St Aloysius' Church; he renewed his acquaintance with this beloved city only to discover that there had been changes. 'I have been up to Godstow this afternoon,' he wrote. 'I am sorry to say the aspens that lined the river are everyone felled.'[80] This gently expressed, deeply felt event of the aspens' felling took shape in the subtle, mesmerizing passion of 'Binsey Poplars'. With its distinct rhythm, haunting echoes and kenning-words, dense with meaning, this poem of lament and memory, rich with an undertow of devotion, invites us to slow down as we read or speak it, to allow the inscape of this scene long past to be absorbed – instressed.

The sense of ownership with which the poem begins (*my* aspens) emphasizes how dear this place had been to Hopkins. From here, words echo and repeat, travel and chase across the page – memories chasing one another out of the past into the present:

> My aspens dear, whose airy cages quelled,
> Quelled or quenched in leaves the leaping sun,
> All felled, felled, are all felled.

'Quelled', 'quelled', 'quenched', 'leaves', 'leaping', 'felled, felled, are all felled' move, rise and fall as if we are following poplars falling from their verdant shady height ('quenched in leaves the leaping sun') towards a wistful, definitive thud: 'all felled, felled, are all felled'. The movement and musicality of this scene are striking, perhaps because the 'voice' of the poem is not Hopkins' own but that of the 'St Winefred's maidens', as he told his friend Bridges in a letter.[81] These voices of his poetic imagination were those of the maidens of the Holy Well of St Winefred, a place beloved by Hopkins and steeped in stories of devotion and love for God, of surrender and grace.[82] So too was there a holy well in Binsey (attached to the ancient church of St Margaret of Antioch), which may have offered reminders of those other well-maidens; reminders of God's presence deeply held within the rich landscape.

'Not one' of these felled aspens has been spared, we hear:

> Not spared, not one
> That dandled a sandalled
> Shadow that swam or sank
> On meadow & river & wind-wandering weed-winding bank.

All at once, we seem to be in a place of memory and imagination; of days Hopkins spent by the river, when light and shade dappled the water from trees that seemed to play with – to 'dandle' – 'a sandalled shadow'. 'Sandalled' paired with 'dandled' adds a lightness to this bright memory, and an immediacy: as if the sandal-shaped shadows of the tall poplars that danced lightly on the river are somehow before us again; or as if the whole riverside is alive again with the shades ('sandalled shadows') of those who played there. For Hopkins though, 'sandal' could also call to mind devotion, with its echoes of stepping on holy ground or the clothing of the faithful. And so, perhaps for a moment, 'Binsey Poplars' seems to hum with God's presence, even in the sadness of a loss now only held in the memories of those who knew this 'meadow & river & wind-wandering weed-winding bank'.

As the poem turns from maiden-voiced memory, it takes on a darker hue:

> O if we but knew what we do
> When we delve or hew —
> Hack and rack the growing green!

In this, we may hear the echoes of Christ ('Father, forgive them, for they do not know what they are doing') and of Adam, lost to paradise, having to 'delve', to till the earth.[83] Here are the new and old Adams brought before us in a lament for God's thoughtlessly treated earth, and the hope of forgiveness in Christ. We 'hack and rack the growing green', says Hopkins, moving quickly from the angry assonance of the language of torture ('hack and rack') to softer, gentler sounds that contrast with their meaning:

> Since country is so tender
> To touch, her being só slender,
> That, like this sleek and seeing ball
> But a prick will make no eye at all,
> Where we, even where we mean
>   To mend her we end her,

As if to emphasize our blindness to all we do, we are offered the shocking image of *being* blinded. But first the sounds invite us to slow down, through stress and pause and gently sibilant sounds ('so tender / To touch, her being só slender'), to underline the fragility of God's earth. This is a world as easily destroyed as the 'sleek and seeing ball' of the human eye, which can become 'no eye at all' through a single action: a single 'prick' that will destroy sight as violently as we can destroy our world. Having been invited to grasp the inscape of a past bucolic scene, it is as if our own 'instressing' of the landscape must also include a raw understanding of the blindness and violence of its destruction, which can be committed with the best of intentions. 'Even where we mean / To mend her,' says Hopkins, 'we end her / When we hew or delve.' All is lost, apart from in the memory and song of the poem, as 'after-comers cannot guess the beauty been'.

All it took, we hear, were 'ten or twelve, only ten or twelve / Strokes' of an axe to cause the havoc that will 'unselve' this turn in the river; that will rob this dappled, shadowed bank and meadow of its 'self' – of its identity. The maiden-voices sing their repeated words as a wistful lullaby:

DAY 28: SATURDAY

> The sweet especial scene,
> Rural scene, a rural scene,
> Sweet especial rural scene.

The scene has gone and will never be known by 'after-comers'; but, somehow, it is in this inscape of a place and a time long lost that the very richness of the poem lies. Both the memory of the scene and its loss have been exquisitely shared with us and woven together into a new and particular inscape all its own. This is an inscape born out of place, memory, poignant loss, devotion and surrender. And to instress this through 'Binsey Poplars' is to discover more of the perils of forgetting: the dangers of becoming 'unselved' if we take no account of our world's and our fragility, and the mix and motley of God's often ignored, never-to-be-forgotten, Christ-filled world.

Day 29

Monday

The Caged Skylark

As a dare-gale skylark scanted in a dull cage,
   Man's mounting spirit in his bone-house, mean house,
      dwells —
   That bird beyond the remembering his free fells;
This in drudgery, day-labouring-out life's age.

Though aloft on turf or perch or poor low stage
   Both sing sometímes the sweetest, sweetest spells,
   Yet both droop deadly sómetimes in their cells
Or wring their barriers in bursts of fear or rage.

Not that the sweet-fowl, song-fowl, needs no rest —
Why, hear him, hear him babble & drop down to his nest,
   But his own nest, wild nest, no prison.

Man's spirit will be flesh-bound, when found at best,
But uncumberèd: meadow-down is not distressed
   For a rainbow footing it nor he for his bónes rísen.

Written in the same season of life as 'God's Grandeur', when God blazed through Hopkins' world in glorious nature, 'The Caged Skylark' invites us into a more dappled vision of God-with-us: more blended than exultant, more muted than explosive and more questioning than unequivocally sparkling with life. At the heart of it, we find a richness of tone, humanity and devotion that invites our open questioning.

'The Caged Skylark' is a blended picture of the daily demands, constraints, soul-music and flashes of exultation at the heart of human life, expressed through a skylark, the freedom and limitations of which may echo and amplify our own experiences. Now a less-seen bird in these islands, the skylark appears more than once in Hopkins' poetry,[84] with its sweet and rhythmic chirping song of rising and falling notes, which seem to echo its own soaring flight. With the feel of a confident musician, so in tune with their instrument that they need not look, need not adapt their movement to the song being sung, the musician-skylark hovers and swoops, a 'dare-gale' bird – the containment of which, in 'The Caged Skylark', speaks to us of life's soarings and limitations.

This is a poem that begins with comparison and contrast, in language that echoes the 'kenning' of Anglo-Saxon poetry, beloved by Hopkins. Words blend incongruously together so that we are invited into a new and textured understanding or 'kenning'. The poem opens with this 'dare-gale' skylark, bold in its riding on the winds but now a faint echo of itself, held within the confines of a 'dull cage'. Then begins a line-by-line comparison with 'mounting spirit' that dwells within each of us: our own 'dare-gale' heart, contained within our physical selves, our 'bone-house'.[85] These first few lines balance and dance, echoing the similarity that Hopkins is exploring; and we might feel, through his words, the constraints of our 'bone-house, mean house' more readily than our life-quickened humanity. The comparison continues between *'that'* and *'this'*, bird and humankind, each lost in their own prisons, somehow alienated from themselves:

> *That* bird beyond the remembering his free fells;
> *This* in drudgery, day-labouring-out life's age.

Held in its 'mean cage', the glorious 'dare-gale skylark' is no longer able to recall its 'free fells': a gentle, airy alliteration hinting at the swooping fells or its own dipping flight so that we are offered a tantalizing sound-glimpse of a bird's lightness, suspended on the currents of the air. As for us in our 'bone-house, mean house', it is as if we, too, have forgotten our creaturely existence: we have been loved into being by God, who holds us in our ordinary and soaring lives. Instead, we seem caught in the simple hard work of daily living; in the relentless march of 'drudgery, day-labouring-out life's age', with its steady, stressed tread towards the grave.

Yet this is not the last word in a life that is both ours and God's within us. Hopkins turns to paint a picture of how we share, with the skylark, joy and loss, fear and anger; living lives more mixed than univocal. From 'that' and 'this', we turn to 'both': both skylark and humanity are filled with joy and are cast low.

> Though aloft on turf or perch or poor low stage
>   Both sing sometímes the sweetest, sweetest spells,
>   Yet both droop deadly sómetimes in their cells
> Or wring their barriers in bursts of fear or rage.

We like the skylark, may sing whether 'aloft' or cast down; and with lingering emphasis, we hear of the '*sweet*est, *sweet*est spells' of our utterance: magical songs of exultation or prayerful incantation. And yet we both 'droop deadly sometimes' in our own prisons or seem to rattle the cages ('wring their barriers') as we rail against confinement. By the end of the octet, we have been gifted a vision of soaring freedom and tight confinement, of joy and of sorrow, and of being caught in daily life in all its limitations, forgetful of our nature. Yet still we are able to speak and sing mysteries in the 'sweetest, sweetest spells' that emerge even in captivity, even in our self-forgetting.

Then the poem shifts to show us subtler differences between the skylark's captivity and our own. In 'hints and guesses', we are offered a deeper vision of our identity as creatures of God:

> Not that the sweet-fowl, song-fowl, needs no rest —
> Why, hear him, hear him babble & drop down to his nest,
>   But his own nest, wild nest, no prison.

DAY 29: MONDAY

It isn't, says the poet, that the 'sweet-fowl, song-fowl' skylark can always be on the wing; but its rest must be of its own choice and in 'his own nest, wild nest, no prison'. We on the other hand, seem to feel our imprisonment more keenly as we forget who we are and who we shall be:

> Man's spirit will be flesh-bound, when found at best,
> But uncumberèd: meadow-down is not distressed
>   For a rainbow footing it nor he for his bónes rísen.

While we might feel keenly the constraints of our creaturely existence – in all its 'drudgery, day-labouring-out' tread – and feel tempted to think of spiritual fulfilment as freedom from our earthbound, captive self, Hopkins offers us a glimpse of a different, profoundly incarnational vision, caught up in God's life here and in eternity. We are, says Hopkins, 'found at best' when 'flesh-bound'; and at the resurrection, with 'bones-risen', we will experience our 'flesh-bound' life as no more cumbersome than a soft meadow experiencing a rainbow. Here is the 'now' of life and the 'not-yet' of God's kingdom and risen life, allowing us to glimpse that – in the fullness of God's kingdom – we may know the deepest embodiment of our humanity, both 'flesh-bound' and 'found at best'.

'The Caged Skylark' offers us a vision of profound integration that holds the whole of us together in our deepest identity as creatures of God: in daily life and soaring heights, body and spirit, present and future. It also shows us something of the paradox of God-gifted life, both free and contained, quickened within our 'bone-house, which is the place of our calling and the fullest incarnation of our God-given humanity. We may be invited, as we walk through Lent, to reflect on Christ's call into the freedom and constraint of his earthly life (with both its drudgery and glory); to reflect on our own freedoms and our strictures; and to remember who we are and who we shall be, as we walk our own rich and complex, provisional, hopeful and fearful lives, caught up in the life of the one who calls us into all life.

Day 30

Tuesday

Let me be to Thee

Let me be to Thee as the circling bird,
Or bat with tender and air-crisping wings
That shapes in half-light his departing rings,
From both of whom a changeless note is heard.
I have found my music in a common word,
Trying each pleasurable throat that sings
And every praised sequence of sweet strings,
And know infallibly which I preferred.

The authentic cadence was discovered late
Which ends those only strains that I approve,
And other science all gone out of date
And minor sweetness scarce made mention of:
I have found the dominant of my range and state —
Love, O my God, to call thee Love and Love.

How do we discover our spiritual home? And how do we know when we have landed in the place of our deepest encounter with Christ, where our hearts are most attuned to the beating heart of our Saviour and his love? This can be a matter of discernment as we chart a way through life, listening for the 'hints and guesses' (to borrow from T. S. Eliot)[86] that lead us on; listening for the echoes and watching for the shapes and shadows that describe to us the contours of our faith.

This discernment, of knowing deeply when and where our hearts are at home, may be more pressing at some times in our lives than at others. And when it is pressing – and if it is pressing at the moment – it may be that Hopkins' youthful, fresh and simple devotional sonnet, circling around his Saviour, can be a north star: one guiding us in its expression of searching and settling; hovering and homing towards a place of resolution, steered by the call of Christ. Written when Hopkins was two years into his time as an undergraduate at Balliol College, Oxford, 'Let me be to Thee' emerged as an expression of his keen and questing faith; it reflects the 'Amen' he spoke at this time of his life, as he discovered his spiritual home.

Here, in this sonnet written soon after leaving the creative sphere of his family life, we find a still-early example of his poetic craftsmanship. Yet to discover his mature, authentic poetic voice, Hopkins nevertheless offers glimpses in his early poems of what was to be; in the beautifully economical 'Let me be to Thee', we find traces of the crafted, disciplined, creative, subtle and exuberant poet he was to become. This is a poem in which compound and invented words are few, and the dynamism of sprung rhythm is yet to appear. Yet there is that blend of structure and conversational authenticity that was to become a hallmark of Hopkins' sonnets: a fusion that communicates dappled life and faith in the natural, shifting cadences of speech, unfettered by the strictures of poetic language, but still held within the poetic form of the sonnet.

The opening line of 'Let me be to Thee' immediately brings us into the orbit of God in a moment of self-offering. The first line, 'Let me be to Thee as the circling bird,' draws us to a sense of supplication and a heart-opening offering to the God who is at the centre of all experience, all life. 'May I hover around you,' Hopkins says, 'like a "circling bird",' calling to mind the flight of the bird drawn to that which it most desires, most wants for nourishment, but not as prey to be devoured. This is the hovering of a bird caught up in warm currents of air, raised by the thermals that sustain its flight, as if hovering and uplifted in the warmth of God's orbit.

The plea goes on in the poet's desire to be that circling creature – bird or bat – that ascends and moves in flickering circles of light, caught in an orbit of belonging, and discovering its own 'changeless note' as if finding the sweetest, matched frequency with the one who holds us in our orbit. With this, the tone and images slightly shift, as the poet recounts the joy of discerning his 'music in a common word' and his search ('trying each pleasurable throat that sings') for song: a melody, a tone to match his own. He has searched and he knows 'infallibly which I preferred':

> I have found my music in a common word,
> Trying each pleasurable throat that sings
> And every praised sequence of sweet strings,
> And know infallibly which I preferred.

The first part of the sonnet has circled and shifted, orbited and hummed and beaten the air around the object of Hopkins' devotion in a quest of faith. And now – as the octet gives way to the final six lines – it is as if the circling bird, with its 'changeless note', lands and settles into what is (for Hopkins) the 'authentic cadence' of his faith, reaching towards a sense of resolution. He is arriving at an amen of completeness and commitment as he discovers an expression of faith to which his heart is attuned and in which he can say that he has:

> found the dominant of my range and state —
> Love, O my God, to call thee Love and Love.

It is now, he says, in finding this 'authentic cadence' and the 'dominant' of his 'range and stage' that his 'music in a common word' can be found and known and spoken. And this is Love, which calls him home, which calls him to this place of resolution:

> Love, O my God, to call thee Love and Love.

'Let me be to Thee' is a poem of the open heart caught in devotion. A heart discerning and held by the frequency of God's call, and enraptured by a sense of homecoming, resolution, devotion and self-offering.

And yet, as we know, arriving at a place of faithful resolution will not be an end to our journeying. We can find ourselves, as Hopkins did, continuing our walk with Christ on a journey of faith in which we are tested and buffeted by the ordinary and extraordinary things of life; by the unexpected discordant notes, the missed beats and half-beats; and by the mysteries of faith and of our own soul.

For Hopkins, the complexities, the exuberance and the pain of subsequent years were largely ahead of him. For now, we rest with him in the devotional beauty of 'Let me be to Thee' and share a moment of stillness – an amen – on the journey of faith.

Day 31

Wednesday

The Sea and the Skylark

On ear and ear two noises too old to end
   Trench—right, the tide that ramps against the shore;
   With a flood or a fall, low lull-off or all roar,
Frequenting there while moon shall wear and wend.

Left hand, off land, I hear the lark ascend,
   His rash-fresh re-winded new-skeinèd score
   In crisps of curl off wild winch whirl, and pour
And pelt music, till none's to spill nor spend.

How these two shame this shallow and frail town!
   How ring right out our sordid turbid time,
Being pure! We, life's pride and cared-for crown,

   Have lost that cheer and charm of earth's past prime:
Our make and making break, are breaking, down
   To man's last dust, drain fast towards man's first slime.

Less than ten miles north of St Beuno's lies Rhyl, a town steeped in history and 'antiquarian interest'. By the 1870s, it had become a tourist destination, a 'fashionable watering place' and 'among the best sea-bathing resorts in the principality'.[87]

Yet if a low-spirited Hopkins hoped that Rhyl might refresh him when he visited in 1877, he was disappointed by the 'shallow and frail town' of 'The Sea and the Skylark' and seemed to find himself caught between visions. On the one hand, he glimpsed a vision of eternity, of God's heartbeat expressed in singing verse in 'The Sea and the Skylark'; on the other hand, he discerned human endeavour, a thin flutter when it forgets the ringing cadence of God.

That the soundscape of 'The Sea and the Skylark' was so important to Hopkins was clear in a letter he wrote to his friend Bridges a few years later. The sonnet was written, he said, 'in my Welsh days, in my salad days, when I was fascinated by *cynghanedd*',[88] that complex 'consonant-chime' of traditional Welsh poetry. Made up of echoes and internal rhymes, of alliteration and shifting vowels nestled in words with similar consonants,[89] so that meaning seems to travel across the page, the influence of *cynghanedd* dances through the language of 'The Sea and the Skylark'.

Hopkins launches into the poem with a wall of sound, catching us up with him in an eternal landscape; a landscape standing between 'two noises' that seem 'too old to end' and that balance and echo each other ('two ... too old to end' and 'on ear and ear'), dancing from side to side in movements of air-borne music. These are sounds that immediately seem so insistent, so ancient that they craft and travel pathways to human mind and heart. In hovering to left and right, ear to ear, they 'trench', which carries overtones of furrowing or leaving an impression, even of laying channels for new shoots of life to emerge. It is as if these sounds both travel time-worn pathways to the soul and lay foundations for new depths of experience; it is as if they create the possibility for us to instress the hum of God's world as it reaches our hearts.

> On ear and ear two noises too old to end
>   Trench—right, the tide that ramps against the shore;
>   With a flood or a fall, low lull-off or all roar,
> Frequenting there while moon shall wear and wend.

The sound that reaches to the right, we soon hear, is that of the sea rising to meet the land and falling away in a susurration of the gentle, forceful movement of its eternal tides to the rhythm of the moon's seasons. We hear, with the poet, the soughing of a tide that 'ramps against the shore' and the deeply resonant near-and-far of 'flood or fall, low lull-off or all roar' of the pounding waves: expressions of the sea's inscape.

From the waves' cry, the poet turns to birdsong on the left of this trenching sound. 'Left hand, off land', we hear (in a blending of echoes, rhymes, vowels and the gentle pacing needed to find our way through the sounds) the cry of the lark breaking the sky, with

> His rash-fresh re-winded new-skeinèd score
> In crisps of curl off wild winch whirl, and pour
> And pelt music, till none's to spill nor spend.

In densely allusive language, with all-the-richer meaning, we hear the cry of the lark as it rises and plunges and flings its own song into the sky 'till none's to spill or spend'. This is the inscape of a bird that, more than simply singing in the sky, seems to be itself when there, in communion with air and sea, land and heavens, 'pour[ing]' out its 'rash-fresh re-winded new-skeinèd score'. Some years later, Hopkins wrote to his friend Bridges about this 'rash-fresh' song, continually ending and beginning, 'without ever losing its first freshness, being a thing both new and old'. He wrote, too, of how lark-song falls from the heavens 'tricklingly or waveringly', like unwound thread falling in curls and coils from 'skein' and 'winch'. 'There is ... plenty meant', he said, and 'dreadful to explain these things in cold blood',[90] especially when he was offering a glimpse of the world engaged with the rhythms of its Creator – unstoppable, ancient and fresh – until the volta.

As the sestet begins (as if turning away from the roaring sea and spendthrift lark, and turning towards the reader and Rhyl), a new tone emerges.

> How these two shame this shallow and frail town!
>   How ring right out our sordid turbid time,
> Being pure! We, life's pride and cared-for crown,

DAY 31: WEDNESDAY

> Have lost that cheer and charm of earth's past prime:
> Our make and making break, are breaking, down
> To man's last dust, drain fast towards man's first slime.

Hopkins laments how the lark and the sea, in their eternal freshness, 'shame this shallow and frail town'. With their beauty a counterpoint, they seem to toll a bell for our 'sordid turbid time': disturbed and murky, confused and unclear. And we, the poet laments, we humans, seemingly the pinnacle of creaturely creation, 'Have lost that cheer and charm of earth's past prime.' We have lost our connection with the intimations of eternity around us, the 'rash-fresh' of the lark or the 'flood' and 'fall' of the ocean, renewed with the moon's seasons. Stressed words ('shame', 'shallow', 'frail', 'ring right', 'sordid', 'turbid') and travelling-sound echoes ('make and making break, are breaking') take us on a spiral of humankind breaking down 'to man's last dust' in our failure to apprehend God's eternal beauty. Hopkins laments our time-bound forgetting of our eternal, eternally present God and shows us the cost of such forgetting.

In 'The Sea and the Skylark', the cost seems to come with a call. For one like Hopkins, the call was to stand in the breach between the brightness of God's eternal glory and the flickering of the passing moment; to lament and bear witness to our easy forgetting. It is a call – shared with us in the language of a poem rich with God's life – to allow God to shape us, rather than our shaping the world with our otherwise impoverished selves. 'The Sea and the Skylark' nudges us towards an instressing of God's eternal presence. Even its final words of lament might nudge us towards a remembering and a rebirth: from breaking down 'to man's last dust', we are offered a hint of moving 'towards man's first slime', with a sense of life beginning afresh, now or in an eternity, which falls even beyond the span of lark-song or lunar sea-season.

Day 32

Thursday

Spring

Nothing is so beautiful as Spring —
   When weeds, in wheels, shoot long and lovely and lush;
   Thrush's eggs look little low heavens, and thrush
Through the echoing timber does so rinse and wring
The ear, it strikes like lightnings to hear him sing;
   The glassy peartree leaves and blooms, they brush
   The descending blue; that blue is all in a rush
With richness; the racing lambs too have fair their fling.

What is all this juice and all this joy?
   A strain of the earth's sweet being in the beginning
In Eden garden. — Have, get, before it cloy,

   Before it cloud, Christ, lord, and sour with sinning,
Innocent mind and Mayday in girl and boy,
   Most, O maid's child, thy choice and worthy the winning.

Spring was magical for Hopkins. He saw 'growth in everything',[91] as the world suddenly became 'word, expression, news of God'.[92] So when, in the particularly wet year of 1877, the world sprang to life around him in the bright freshness of a saturated landscape, vivid green in its lush beauty, it was perhaps no surprise that Hopkins wrote the poem 'Spring'.

'Spring' is a poem of burgeoning life: one which seems to capture Hopkins' sense that the world shows us paradise and fall together; and shows us the blend of grace and folly, gift and loss that shape our humanity. This runs through the poem as surely as the sprung rhythm that, vivid with emphasis and movement, drives the poem forward, as though the sonnet form can barely contain the sense of spring growth. Yet there is a poignancy here because, in 'Spring', there is also an expression of life in all its bounty, just before it spills over into decay: spring before it spills into summer, into autumn; and human freshness before it spills into a knowingness that robs of us of innocence. Matching this movement, the tone shifts from the octet – with its lyrical image and soundscape that share with us spring's unique inscape – to the more urgent, rapid, slightly breathless tone of the sestet, which moves us towards an anxious appeal to Christ to catch the dropping, over-ripening fruit before it passes its freshest.

Before this, though, the poem has begun with the emphatic cry of joy: 'Nothing is so beautiful as Spring', when even 'weeds [not known for their beauty], in wheels, shoot long and lovely and lush'. Here, we have the unmistakably open, breathless and expansive sounds ('when', 'weeds', 'wheels') of new growth. Tendrils of fresh shoots unfurl their tightly circled selves and seem to elongate to become '*long* and *lovely* and *lush*', bringing before us the inscape of spring growth in its unquenchable reaching towards the world. Then, as if in a reminder of the vastness as well as the particularity of God's world, the heavens in miniature are brought before us and the air fills with sound:

> Thrush's eggs look little low heavens, and thrush
> Through the echoing timber does so rinse and wring
> The ear, it strikes like lightnings to hear him sing;

The blue-shaded, speckled-surfaced thrush eggs look like 'little low heavens': small earth-bound pictures of starlit sky. And the sound of the thrush seems to join heaven and earth, weaving through the 'echoing timber' of the woodland in sounds that 'rinse and wring the ear'. This is birdsong that seems to flow within us, cleansing as it 'rinses' and 'wrings'; so sharp and bright that 'it strikes like lightnings to hear him sing'. Not lightning but 'lightnings', as if the sound strikes over and over again, with a vivid clarity. Heaven and earth also seem to meet in the shiny leaves and flowers of the pear tree, which 'brush / The descending blue'; and 'that blue', adds the poet, with an emphatic repetition, 'is all in a rush / With richness'.

> The glassy peartree leaves and blooms, they brush
> The descending blue; that blue is all in a rush
> With richness; the racing lambs too have fair their fling.

This is God's world in which heaven and earth touch in green growth reaching to meet the blueness of the 'little low' heavens and the 'descending blue' of the sky; and all is flecked with an effervescent whiteness of blossom and 'racing lambs'. Sound, colour and movement are so entwined that we seem to instress spring's vivid inscape and inhabit God's blended world of heaven and earth, earth and heaven. And then the tone shifts.

'What is all this juice and joy?' The poet is asking, 'What does all this lush new life mean?' before an answer emerges, with a 'simplicity' that, says one writer on Hopkins, is the poem's 'strength and its weakness':[93]

> What is all this juice and all this joy?
>   A strain of the earth's sweet being in the beginning
> In Eden garden.

Spring's lush bounty, it seems, recalls earth's innocence: its 'sweet being in the beginning'. For some, this is 'moving and powerful'; but for others, this seems an 'incomplete, naïve' answer to such a question.[94] We may find ourselves leaning one way or another in our response. Or we may find ourselves drawn less towards the simplicity of the answer than towards the richness of the following lines. These seem to carry us beyond the innocence of Eden and into a haunting and challenging landscape, shot through with faith and hope and yearning, in a plea for Christ to catch up the whole of creation in this 'strain of the earth's sweet being in the beginning'.

DAY 32: THURSDAY

> Have, get, before it cloy,
>
> Before it cloud, Christ, lord, and sour with sinning,
> Innocent mind and Mayday in girl and boy,
>   Most, O maid's child, thy choice and worthy the winning.

We are no sooner shown this 'strain' (this distant relative) of Eden pouring through God's world (rather than the *stain* of a fallen world) than we find ourselves in a hurried prayer for this glimpse of paradise to be caught up by Christ before it loses its lustre; before the innocence of the young, their 'Mayday', is 'sour[ed] with sinning'. These are poignant and curious lines, at once hurried ('have, get, before … / Before') but also hesitant, with pauses breaking up lines of relaxed longer sounds ('sour with sinning'). It is as if, in this faltering urgency, we are invited into the emotional landscape of life made precious by its inevitable passing. We hold on and we hurry up; we slow down and we savour, all at once, as we discover the vagaries of the gift, grace, innocence and decay of the world.

At the last, in 'Spring', Hopkins' plea is for the freshness of open-hearted innocence to be caught up by the Incarnate One, who saves and savours us, and for whom humanity 'in girl and boy' is 'worthy the winning' by Christ, the 'maid's child'. Life's journey will go on, freshness will be lost, and Spring will overbalance into summer – into autumn. And yet for a season, we may find that we are able to open out our dappled hearts to be nurtured and transformed by the presence of God-with-us in Christ, the 'maid's child', in the saving and transformation of a world that still bears the traces of paradise.

Day 33

Friday

Ribblesdale

Earth, sweet Earth, sweet landscape, with leavès throng
And louchèd low grass, heaven that dost appeal
To, with no tongue to plead, no heart to feel;
That canst but only be, but dost that long—

Thou canst but be, but that thou well dost; strong
Thy plea with him who dealt, nay does now deal,
Thy lovely dale down thus and thus bids reel
Thy river, and o'er gives all to rack or wrong.

And what is Earth's eye, tongue, or heart else, where
Else, but in dear and dogged man?—Ah, the heir
To his own selfbent so bound, so tied to his turn,

To thriftless reave both our rich round world bare
And none reck of world after, this bids wear
Earth brows of such care, care and dear concern.

In 1882, Hopkins is teaching Latin and Greek at Stonyhurst College in the heart of north-west England. Some years have passed since his 'salad days'[95] at St Beuno's; his many moves since then have taken him far from its beautiful, sometimes-brooding, sometimes-protective landscape. He has experienced the bleak wretchedness of great industrial towns, vibrant but soul-crushing places that brought life and courted death. He has ministered among people labouring through smog and

DAY 33: FRIDAY

poverty; he has walked streets tinged with manufacturing's dark patina. All of these have shaped him and now, in 'Ribblesdale', his first sonnet for two years, Hopkins lays out before us both the beauty of the countryside and the shades of the town in this strangely prescient, gentle and tough poem, with its plea to honour God's world.

Flowing through Yorkshire and Lancashire to the coast, the River Ribble reflects the centuries of human life along its course, blending its own story with ours as it travels through sweet country air and the pall and grit of pollution. For Hopkins, this seemed to give Ribblesdale a particular inscape that transcended time while being part of it, bearing the beauty and the scars of his own time and also caught in the birth-pangs of a world awaiting God's kingdom. 'For the creation waits with eager longing for the revealing of the children of God,' as Hopkins quoted in a manuscript version of the poem, as if to underline this.[96] All of this makes for an unusually dynamic inscape to a place both in-time and out of time, caught up in both our mottled human story and God's generative life.

'Ribblesdale' shifts and changes in mood as it unfolds. This 'Earth, sweet Earth, sweet landscape', crowded and busy with leaves that 'throng', mutely appeals to heaven:

> Earth, sweet Earth, sweet landscape, with leavès throng
> And louchèd low grass, heaven that dost appeal
> To, with no tongue to plead, no heart to feel;
> That canst but only be, but dost that long—

'Louchèd', Hopkins said later, was a word he coined to suggest 'slouched' or 'slouching'.[97] This singular word, with its many associations, might bring to mind the languor of lazily unfolding countryside, with slouching, low-lying grass or velvety hills. Other associations might come to mind: in 'throng / And louchèd', we might see the shades of industrial towns, peopled with slouched, oppressed souls – as voiceless as Ribblesdale, which has 'no tongue to plead'. Neither does it have a 'heart to feel'; and though we know the literal truth of this, these words still strike a strangely discordant note. This voiceless, heartless landscape appeals to heaven simply by being, as we are told twice, with an emphatic repetition; but we have to wait to discover the nature of this appeal.

> That canst but only be, but dost that long—
>
> Thou canst but be, but that thou well dost; strong
> Thy plea with him who dealt, nay does now deal,
> Thy lovely dale down thus and thus bids reel
> Thy river, and o'er gives all to rack or wrong.

'That canst but only be … / Thou canst but be.' It may be tempting to think of this as the dale 'being' itself in some 'pure' form – beautiful, bucolic, grand and brooding – but the swirling sense, which is emerging, is that for the dale to 'be' itself is far more complex. The unique character – the inscape – of this dale is that of a place shaped by its Creator and by its story, by earth and humanity. So the dale makes its plea to God the Creator who 'dealt' its life force and still deals it ('does now deal') as sustainer. God still 'bids reel' – still causes the river's flow through the dale – but so too is God present in all the gone-wrongness in the dale, in all that has been 'o'er give[n] … to rack or wrong': God, it seems, does not eradicate all that prevents our world's flourishing; but he does lie at its heart. What further plea can be made by this voiceless, voluble dale, bearing the mark of its Creator and of humanity? The final six lines draw out for us the only possible plea to make:

> And what is Earth's eye, tongue, or heart else, where
> Else, but in dear and dogged man?—Ah, the heir
> To his own selfbent so bound, so tied to his turn,
>
> To thriftless reave both our rich round world bare
> And none reck of world after, this bids wear
> Earth brows of such care, care and dear concern.

DAY 33: FRIDAY

Where else can we find the means of caring for this landscape, shot through with the scars of humanity and history, than through 'dear and dogged man?' It is, says Hopkins, for us to give voice to the cry of the earth and make a plea on its behalf; but we are 'selfbent': turned in towards our own concerns. We are 'so bound', 'so tied' to our daily round and to our heedless and extravagant plundering of our 'rich round world' that we take no heed of what is to come after us ('none reck of this world after').

There is a profound challenge here to our blindness and folly and to our misguided focus on what seems to matter as we forge progress, while the earth mutely cries; and God calls on *us* to call on *him*. Yet there is also a deep tenderness and compassion in these final lines. Even in our 'thriftless', 'selfbent' state we are not roundly condemned; we are 'dear and dogged', beloved in our determination to craft a life. Even God's earth, God's Ribblesdale, though silent and dependent on us, looks on with pity and 'wear[s] / ... brows of such care, care and dear concern'. This same 'sweet Earth, sweet landscape' of the opening lines now looks with compassion on those who shape its life for good and ill.

It is 1882. In the years that have passed since Hopkins knew the unalloyed grandeur of God in his surroundings, he has seen the gift and the cost of our human ingenuity and endeavour. Now, in 'Ribblesdale', he calls us to awaken from our forgetting of God's gifts. But this is more than a call to repent: it is also a call to know ourselves as beloved creatures of God; to look with compassion on the dappled blend of folly, love and care with which we shape God's world; and to speak for the silent landscape.

Day 34

Saturday

Repeat That, Repeat

Repeat that, repeat,
Cuckoo, bird, and open ear wells, heart-springs, delightfully sweet,
With a ballad, with a ballad, a rebound
Off trundled timber and scoops of the hillside ground,
   hollow hollow hollow ground:
The whole landscape flushes on a sudden at a sound.

Holy Week begins soon. This may be a time to pause and to listen, in a moment of quiet, to God's world before we travel towards the Cross and beyond. This is an instant for a brief reflection on a brief poem.

In 'Repeat That, Repeat', Hopkins has gifted us just a few lines that explore the power and beauty of sound in the landscape. They invite us to pause and to hear the sounds that we may miss in the press of life. They also offer us a glimpse of the remarkable inscape of this poet of inscapes, who heard so clearly and gazed so deeply into God's world, instressing the pulsing of God's life and sharing it with us. Repeat that, repeat again and we shall hear how life pours forth; not in regulation, curated formal verse but in echoes and reverberations.

The poem begins with an invitation to a bird to repeat its song, to 'cuckoo' into the world; and in this verb, though the bird may or may not be a cuckoo, we immediately hear its airy, haunting two-toned cry, which seems to float over the landscape. The bird's repetition 'open[s] ear wells'; or perhaps the repetition of a birdsong causes any open ear to 'well' in response, as if rising to meet the sound. 'Ear *wells*' and 'heart-*springs*, delightfully sweet' as sound floods through bird and listener, a spring of living water; or, in an echo of 'heartstrings', teases hearts gently into life.

The bird's song continues to tell its tune afresh over and over again, 'with a ballad, with a ballad', echoing and glancing off 'trundled timber'. With its own alliterative repetition, 'trundled timber' might conjure an ancient landscape of woodland that has flowed and moved over centuries, providing a place for birdsong to resonate, rebound and fill the air, just as the song swoops and glances off the hillsides' 'hollow hollow hollow ground'. It has happened for timeless years and yet it seems to happen in a moment: the bird casts its song into the air; the 'landscape flushes'. It seems to respond and rise to meet the birdsong, brought suddenly to life and somehow brighter, as if suffused with the blood of a rich heartbeat: all through the landscape-filling sound of a single bird.

In this poet's song of a bird's song rapturously poured into God's world, the landscape is changed as we can be changed 'on a sudden' by the sights, sounds and glimpses of God that we miss or take for granted. It might only be in stilling ourselves in a moment of quiet that they break upon us, surprising us, opening our hearts to the pulse of God's life around us.

In this moment, we can linger ahead of Holy Week and listen to the pulses of God's world, knowing that this is the place which bore his son, and which drew his son through the Passion and into death and beyond.

Repeat that, repeat.

Day 35

Monday

To Seem the Stranger

To seem the stranger lies my lot, my life
Among strangers. Father and mother dear,
Brothers and sisters are in Christ not near
And he my peace / my parting, sword and strife.

England, whose honour O all my heart woos, wife
To my creating thought, would neither hear
Me, were I pleading, plead nor do I: I wear-
Y of idle a being but by where wars are rife.

I am in Ireland now; now I am at a thírd
Remove. Not but in all removes I can
Kind love both give and get. Only what word

Wisest my heart breeds dark heaven's baffling ban
Bars or hell's spell thwarts. This to hoard unheard,
Heard unheeded, leaves me a lonely began.

Lent is drawing to its close. As we come closer to the Passion, we may find ourselves entering more deeply into the final days suffered by Christ towards the end of his earthly life: days of betrayal and loss and profound suffering. That he knew the depths of human sorrow in those final days, we can be certain; that he knew loneliness and rejection, we can be sure; and towards the very end, he knew the overwhelming isolation of being unaccompanied in Gethsemane and unheeded on the Cross.

As we enter these final days, we turn towards one of Hopkins' most profound poems of loss and suffering and isolation.

'To Seem the Stranger' (one of his 'Terrible Sonnets') shares the pain of a soul, rooted in faith, who also knows his own sorrows and is not willing to pretend his way out of them. The poem's dominant notes are alienation and isolation, expressed with subtle intensity through Hopkins' characteristic echoes and repetitions, alliteration and 'vowelling':[98] sound travels and flows as words tumble and invert across the page. All of this brings before us the paradoxically unmissable howl of one who is struggling to be heard.

Written during his final years living in Dublin, 'To Seem the Stranger' shares the isolation of one living 'at a thírd / Remove' from all that is familiar and beloved. He travelled and wrote and had acquaintances and colleagues during this time; but this was, for him, a 'wretched life' of 'wasted years'. He could still say, with passion, that his life was 'inwardly' and 'most visibly and outwardly shaped by Christ's'; but he struggled with 'helplessness and weakness' and with the 'work assigned to [him]' during his years in Dublin. 'All my undertakings miscarry,' he wrote in notes made on retreat. 'Oh my God, look down on me.'[99]

The octet lays out Hopkins' situation in stark terms. 'To seem the stranger,' he begins in a series of stressed alliterations, 'lies my lot, my life / Among strangers,' emphasizing his grinding isolation and his state of – what? Of feeling himself to *be* a stranger to others? Of feeling that he is *becoming stranger* or perhaps feeling that he is increasingly a stranger to himself. The words may circle around all these meanings, all held together in the repeated sounds 'seem', 'stranger', 'strangers', which surround the languorous 'lies my lot, my life'. These repetitions and pauses cause us to slow down; and as we do so, we find ourselves between 'strangers' – somehow caught with Hopkins in his 'lot' and 'among strangers'.

> To seem the stranger lies my lot, my life
> Among strangers. Father and mother dear,
> Brothers and sisters are in Christ not near
> And he my peace / my parting, sword and strife.

Family is far away, separated by the sea and by denomination if not faith: they are 'in Christ not near'. Apart from those he loves most, Hopkins finds himself alone and isolated even in following his life-shaping calling to follow Christ: 'my peace / my parting, sword and strife'. 'Peace' and 'parting' seem so closely allied that they are separated by no more than an oblique, as if the flip side of each other; and the poet echoes Jesus' words of coming not to bring peace but division.[100] For Hopkins, in a twist of faith and feeling, there is both peace and division with Jesus: his all-in-all and his 'sword and strife'.

As the octet goes on, the poet's sense of loss deepens. His memory drifts to England, his homeland and 'wife' to his 'creating thought'. And his plaintive cry ('O') in the midst of more open sounds invites us into the rhythm of a heart lost in sighs of yearning, breath stopping and starting. He fears that, now, the land that sparked life and poetry would no longer hear him if he cried out; and he will not cry out:

> England, whose honour O all my heart woos, wife
> To my creating thought, would neither hear
> Me, were I pleading, plead nor do I: I wear-
> Y of idle a being but by where wars are rife.

The octet ends with a line that is both long in tone and condensed in meaning. 'Weary' is so drawn out across lines that we cannot help but grasp the long-drawn-out-bone-wrenching weariness, which seems rooted in being 'idle' in a place where 'wars are rife'. More overworked than 'idle', Hopkins might have been alluding to his sense of being 'of little or no use'[101] at a time of change and unrest; and at a time when his muse seems to have left him.

The final lines, the sestet, take us still further into the poet's sense of isolation. 'I am in Ireland now', he says, 'now I am at a thírd / Remove': removed from country; removed from his family and from his dearest friends. There are also other possible removes: from the faith of his upbringing, from his order back home, from the God who seems distant and from his own peace. But perhaps the greatest 'remove' is from his own words and of feeling unheard. Now, in paradoxically rich and expressive language, he speaks out the anguish of *not*-speaking and not being heard:

> Only what word
>
> Wisest my heart breeds dark heaven's baffling ban
> Bars or hell's spell thwarts. This to hoard unheard,
> Heard unheeded, leaves me a lonely began.

Hopkins' painful lament is that even the wisest words his heart nurtures or births – whether poetry or prayer – remain unspeakable and unspoken. They seem to be barred by 'heaven's baffling ban'; either that or they are thwarted by 'hell's spells'. Heaven or hell: Hopkins is not sure which. There is a familiarity to this conundrum: in the very human struggle to discern the source and purpose of our suffering, we question the goodness of the God we trust. We turn in circles and test our thoughts as if to find an anchor for our hearts, just as Hopkins does in his unpunctuated, punching 'dark heaven's baffling ban / Bars or hell's spells thwarts': words that seem bent on forcing their way through 'ban' and 'spell' to be heard.

The poem leaves us with a final turn, ironically with a verbal dexterity and poignancy that belies the apparent struggle to speak. Hopkins' 'hoard unheard, / heard unheeded' – what he is unable to share and what he shares with no response (whether poetry or prayer) – leave him a 'lonely began'; stripped bare, it seems, as if ending a life both complete and incomplete, with the merest hint of being ready to begin again.

We have found Hopkins at the depths of his isolation. Yet the faithful air that he breathes still seeps through his words. He still knows Christ as the one who calls him, as his 'peace' and his 'parting', his 'sword' and his 'strife'.

The end of Lent is coming but it is not yet here. We find ourselves, with Hopkins, on the brink of 'a lonely began'.

Day 36

Tuesday

No Worst

No worst, there is none. Pitched past pitch of grief,
More pangs will, schooled at forepangs, wilder wring.
Comforter, where, where is your comforting?
Mary, mother of us, where is your relief?
My cries heave, herds-long; huddle in a main, a chief
Woe, wórld-sorrow; on an áge-old anvil wince and sing —
Then lull, then leave off. Fury had shrieked 'No lingering! Let me be fell: force I must be brief'.
O the mind, mind has mountains; cliffs of fall
Frightful, sheer, no-man-fathomed. Hold them cheap
May who ne'er hung there. Nor does long our small
Durance deal with that steep or deep. Here! creep,
Wretch, under a comfort serves in a whirlwind: all
Life death does end and each day dies with sleep.

In this most profound time of sorrow, with intimations of an Easter sunrise still misted and embryonic, we find ourselves again in the pangs of the 'Terrible Sonnets': Hopkins' desolate, intense and intimate cries of pain, which wove through 1885. These are the dark-lands, where we may enter the ruptured, sunless, comfortless place of abandonment; where there is no relief, but for the sleep of death.

These are poems that echo the voices of myriad God-seekers who have cried their pain into the world; and in 'No Worst', we find perhaps the nadir and summit of inner agony. Here, we find the depths of a grief beyond grief and a world-sorrow that seems without comfort, but for the comfort of sleep.

DAY 36: TUESDAY

The broad movement of this sonnet takes us through a landscape of profound suffering, pointing us first inwards, then outwards, then inwards again; and along the way, we seem to hover on the edge of an abyss, in the agonizing possibility of a fall. This threat of suffering is somehow suggested even in the first line that has given this poem its title. With no preamble and so seeming to begin out of nowhere, we hear that 'worst, there is none'. These words seem to hover between 'there is nothing worse' than some unnamed moment, and 'there is no such thing as worst, because there is always something worse': there is always greater suffering, of which we are given only intimations.

> No worst, there is none. Pitched past pitch of grief,
> More pangs will, schooled at forepangs, wilder wring.

From the double, emphatic stress on 'no' and 'none', we move towards the plosives and the single-syllable words that pepper the whole sonnet, deepening its intensity. The words 'pitched past pitch of grief' feel punched into the air: they may suggest the hurl of something 'pitched' or thrown in a moment of grief and rage; or the unique frequency or 'pitch' of grief; or the viscous darkness, the pitch-black of grief; or the tilting or sharpness of grief. But these are 'forepangs' of greater 'pangs' that will be 'wilder wrung', for which there is no comfort and from which there is no relief:

> Comforter, where, where is your comforting?
> Mary, mother of us, where is your relief?

In the poet's pleas, we may hear echoes of the final anguish and a turn towards Mary at the Cross, no longer able to offer a mother's help; no longer able to offer a mother's relief to a suffering child.

The second half of the octet turns Hopkins – and us – back within, towards a soundscape of suffering:

My cries heave, herds-long; huddle in a main, a chief
Woe, wórld-sorrow; on an áge-old anvil wince and sing —
Then lull, then leave off. Fury had shrieked 'No lingering! Let me be fell: force I must be brief'.

Hopkins' cries 'heave', 'wince' and 'sing', and 'shriek', 'lull' and 'leave' as the sound of suffering courses through the insistent stresses and bounces across alliterations, before falling into silence. His cries 'heave, herds-long', with the mournful quality of cattle lowing *en masse* – a herd's-worth uttering the 'woe' of a 'wórld-sorrow'. Cries 'wince and sing' on an 'ágeold anvil', with the sharpness of whetted metal, as if forged in inner agony; but then the sounds 'lull, then leave off'.

As if out of a moment of peace and silence, the mood changes in the sestet as Hopkins contemplates the mind's abyss:

O the mind, mind has mountains; cliffs of fall
Frightful, sheer, no-man-fathomed. Hold them cheap
May who ne'er hung there. Nor does long our small
Durance deal with that steep or deep.

In 'the mind, mind has mountains', we might hear a plaintive repetition, as if to bring to our attention the suffering mind. Or we might hear 'the mind, remember, has mountains': the mind has its dangers; we are taken into a dangerous landscape in which the fall of an anticipated drop is 'frightful, sheer'. In the same way that there is 'no worst', the mind's mountains are 'no-man-fathomed': they can barely be grasped by any who has 'ne'er hung there', on the edge of such an abyss. Finally, we are drawn towards a strange huddling for safety and comfort beneath the worst of life's torments.

Here! creep,
Wretch, under a comfort serves in a whirlwind: all
Life death does end and each day dies with sleep.

Whether 'wretch' is self-lacerating or merely descriptive is unclear. But we are brought at the last towards an uncanny semblance of safety; a sense that here, at the heart of a storm, we may 'sit it out' and, like Job, hear from God in the whirlwind, a place of both suffering and revelation.[102]

Good Friday will have a certain finality to it. We know that Easter Day will come; but we are called to this Holy Week experience of finality for Easter to overwhelm us with the joy of the resurrection. And so, we wait. We wait with Christ in a place of suffering and are reminded that, for Christ, the abandonment and horror of the abyss will end in earthly death. We are called to 'creep' into the heart of the whirlwind to find the comfort-sleep that ends, for us, the darkest week of worship. We are called to know that sitting with suffering is sometimes all that is possible and that, in this place, we may hear the voice of God.

Day 37

Wednesday

The Starlight Night

> Look at the stars! look, look up at the skies!
>   O look at all the fire-folk sitting in the air!
>   The bright boroughs, the circle-citadels there!
> Down in dim woods the diamond delves! the elves'-eyes!
> The grey lawns cold where gold, where quickgold lies!
>   Wind-beat whitebeam! airy abeles set on a flare!
>   Flake-doves sent floating forth at a farmyard scare!
> Ah well! it is all a purchase, all is a prize.
>
> Buy then! bid then! — What? — Prayer, patience, alms, vows.
> Look, look: a May-mess, like on orchard boughs!
>   Look! March-bloom, like on mealed-with-yellow sallows!
> These are indeed the barn; withindoors house
> The shocks. This piece-bright paling shuts the spouse
>   Christ home, Christ and his mother and all his hallows.

It is late on a starlit winter night in 1877 in the depths of North Wales. The sky, free from human light, is populated by the immensity of the stars winking and flickering in the blackness; and for the one who sees deeply into the night, this is a source of wonder and the inspiration of 'The Starlight Night'.

At first glance, peppered with exclamation marks, this winter-written poem might appear simple in its overwhelming, heart-pounding sense of celebration. Densely evocative, meaning-making kenning words ('circle-citadels', 'elves'-eyes', 'wind-beat') scatter light in the night's dark. But this is also a poem that shifts and circles; and a slow reading of it – teasing out its sounds, rhythm and meaning – may draw us towards a new vision of being enfolded in God's glory through the startling brightness of the starlit sky.

Written very shortly after Hopkins wrote 'God's Grandeur' and around the time of a total lunar eclipse, 'The Starlight Night' is another poem born in the season of Lent. Like 'God's Grandeur', it shows us both the glories of God and that mist of unseeing and forgetting which can cloud our hearts as much as our vision. The poem begins, though, with a breathless sense of urgency and excitement, as we are invited to

Look at the stars! look, look up at the skies!
O look at all the fire-folk sitting in the air!

Immediately, we see a sky shot through with the brilliance of 'fire-folk' stars, which have a sense of the faery world about them. Whole worlds lie in the skies, 'bright boroughs' and 'circle-citadels', as if reflecting to us our earth-light of towns and cities. And as the verse goes on, we seem to flicker between earth and the heavens. 'Down in dim woods', says the poet, 'the diamond delves! the elves'-eyes', taking us to firefly-lights flickering in earthly groves. Or perhaps we are taken to the inky interstellar spaces in the heavens, drawn onwards into the deep, velvet darkness of receding woods at night by the diamond light of the stars – 'elves'-eyes'.

Light and dark draw us further on and we catch a glimpse in the ink-blackness of the 'quickgold' of the stars lying on the grass: the fluid shifting reflection of starlight moving through the night sky. Or this might conjure for us 'quickgold' mining, delving deeply into the earth with mercury, as a counterpoint to that other Mercury in the heavens. Still the stars pour through the skies; they are like

Wind-beat whitebeam! airy abeles set on a flare!
Flake-doves sent floating forth at a farmyard scare!

THE STARLIGHT NIGHT

The stars are like whitebeam and abele (white pine) trees, with their star-like whiteness of flower or leaf cast onto the winds ('set on a flare'); they are doves, like airborne white flakes, scared into the sky by events on earth. These are white-silver images, shuttling between heaven and earth, breaking the darkness with gentle, fluid, explosive light as the glory of the heavens breaks upon us. Time and again, we have a picture of light playing in darkness, of the movement between heaven and earth. We are invited to be more than observers: to be at the heart of the starlight night – participants in its movements.

Then the tone shifts, albeit briefly, from wonder to a shocking flatness. 'Ah well!' we hear, 'it is all purchase, all is a prize'. In an echo of his barely earlier poem, 'God's Grandeur', Hopkins hints that even this heavenly gift of starlight can be obscured in a cloud of forgetting by the obsessions of the age. 'It is all a purchase, all is a prize,' the words echo, with a weary emphasis on 'all'. Here, there is no breathless excitement, no exclamation mark; there is instead the poignancy of how easily our vision thins and dims; and God's gift and grace seem to fade from our view. Then the tone shifts again.

Suddenly we are called out of our sadness, out of that flatness of forgetting, towards a different currency which will subvert the 'purchase' and the 'prize'; we are called to our life, our eyes opened afresh to God's goodness. In a breathless stop-start of words, as if we are waking up ('What?'), we are called to 'prayer, patience, alms, vows'. We are called to 'look, look' and to see, to instress, the glory of God in the 'May-mess' of stars bursting into life like spring blossom or the 'March-bloom' of the pussy-willows ('sallows'), releasing the yellow dust of starlight in their slipstream.

> Buy then! bid then! — What? — Prayer, patience, alms, vows.
> Look, look: a May-mess, like on orchard boughs!
>   Look! March-bloom, like on mealed-with-yellow sallows!
> These are indeed the barn; withindoors house
>   The shocks. This piece-bright paling shuts the spouse
>   Christ home, Christ and his mother and all his hallows.

DAY 37: WEDNESDAY

The final lines of the sonnet are perhaps the most curious and richest of all, gathering and scattering meaning as the stars scatter light in the night sky. If we are called to shake ourselves out of our forgetting and to see God's beauty and greatness in the night sky, we may also be called to see more deeply: to discover that the starlight sky is only a shadow of something far greater. These stars are, says the poet, 'indeed the barn': they contain within them ('withindoors') the 'shocks' of wheat[103] of God's harvest. They are the 'piece-bright paling'; they are a light-dappled boundary about God's earth, which 'shuts the spouse' – which holds the space where God, incarnate in Christ, finds a home: 'Christ and his mother and all his hallows'. All the souls and saints who have flickered and lived are still and will always be held fast by Christ in this vision of eternity.

'The Starlight Night', a poem born in Lent, began with a call to look at the skies in sheer wonder at so great a beauty. It leaves us, through a call to awaken from our forgetting, with a grander and more intimate vision; it leaves us, through prayer and patience, with heaven and earth come together: the 'firefolk' and 'hallows'. Look, we are told, and with prayer and patience, we shall see.

Day 38

Maundy Thursday

Spelt from Sibyl's Leaves

Earnest, earthless, equal, attuneable, | vaulty, voluminous, … stupendous
Evening strains to be tíme's vást, | womb-of-all, home-of-all, hearse-of-all night.
Her fond yellow hornlight wound to the west, | her wild hollow hoarlight hung to the height
Waste; her earliest stars, earl-stars, | stárs principal, overbend us,
Fíre-féaturing heaven. For earth | her being has unbound, her dapple is at end, as-
Tray or aswarm, all throughther, in throngs; | self ín self steepèd and pashed—qúite
Disremembering, dísmembering | àll now. Heart, you round me right
With: Óur évening is over us; óur night | whélms, whélms, ánd will end us.
Only the beak-leaved boughs dragonish | damask the tool-smooth bleak light; black,
Ever so black on it. Óur tale, óur oracle! | Lét life, wáned, ah lét life wind
Off hér once skéined stained véined varíety | upon, áll on twó spools; párt, pen, páck
Now her áll in twó flocks, twó folds—black, white; | right, wrong; reckon but, reck but, mind
But thése two; wáre of a wórld where bút these | twó tell, each off the óther; of a rack

DAY 38: MAUNDY THURSDAY

> Where, selfwrung, selfstrung, sheathe- and shelterless, |
> thóughts agaínst thoughts ín groans grínd.

Maundy Thursday is upon us. This is a night of friendship and service and giving thanks. It is a night of love and betrayal; of wrestling, of agony, of being swallowed by coming darkness. This is the night of God's progress through the bleakest of human agonies. Easter Day lies ahead of us; but for now, we are called to enter the dying light of Maundy Thursday and the terrors of the next few hours.

If not a Maundy Thursday poem, 'Spelt from Sibyl's Leaves' is a poem of dappled evening giving way to the darkest of nights that threatens to overwhelm the light; and it is shot through with an anguish that may be the anguish of Gethsemane. Only gradually, and perhaps uncertainly, does the poem resolve into a final vision which blends all that has gone before to take us through and beyond the bounds of mortal life. Seen variously as a poem of judgement, as an exploration of conscience or as a reflection of the experience of damned souls, 'Spelt' has, at its heart, a profound confrontation with what it might mean to be separated from the love of God. As we linger over it, as Hopkins asks us to (this is a poem that needs to be read aloud, with 'long rests' and 'long dwells on the rhyme', he said[104]), we may find that the patterning of language – in breaks, pauses, echoes, travelling sounds and scattered fragments – calls us to slow down, to allow this vivid patchwork of a sonnet to meet us and confront us.

Begun soon after Hopkins arrived in Dublin and two years in the writing, this 'longest ... ever made' sonnet[105] scatters words before us, mimicking the sibyl (or seer) of its title; this sibyl's practice was randomly to choose portents that had been written on leaves.[106] Sounds and words spin from one to another throughout this poem, which defies any straightforward line by line storytelling. We are offered instead glimpses, colours and sounds that collapse time and eternity; that take us through an evening falling into night; and that blend with earthly time falling into the end times, with all its terrors.

The poem begins in mystery, with a flow of apparently disconnected, strewn words. If they are held together, it is by the patterning of sound and cadence as echoing rhymes and alliteration draw us on through:

> Earnest, earthless, equal, attuneable, | vaulty, voluminous, ... stupendous
> Evening strains to be tíme's vást, | womb-of-all, home-of-all, hearse-of-all night.
> Her fond yellow hornlight wound to the west, | her wild hollow hoarlight hung to the height
> Waste; her earliest stars, earl-stars, | stárs principal, overbend us,
> Fíre-féaturing heaven.

It is only in the second line that we learn these words allude to 'evening', a moment in time that is somehow suspended and bigger than itself. It is an arch above the earth ('vaulty') and covering all things. Then as if the poet is lost for words, after a pause, we hear that 'stupendous / Evening strains' to break its own boundaries and expand beyond a single moment to become the all-encompassing container of all there is. It is 'tíme's vást' container through our beginnings ('womb-of-all'), our lives ('home-of-all') and towards our endings: our 'hearse-of-all night'. Throughout this all-embracing evening is light. There is the soft buttery glow of light cast by the horn windows of an old lantern; the ancient greyness of 'wild hollow hoarlight'; and the light of stars travelling across the sky, leaning into the evening from a 'fire-featuring heaven'. Then the tone of the poem shifts.

As evening light fades, the earth herself seems to enter a new phase in which 'her dapple is at an end': as if all the varied colours of day, which exist together and side by side, plunge and mingle all together, 'all throughther, in throngs'. We may be left with an impression of day's colours resolving into a dark and undifferentiated dusk in which even 'self' (the earth's self or our individual human self) is 'ín self steepèd and pashed'.

DAY 38: MAUNDY THURSDAY

Perhaps this is a self that is lost in its own self ('ín self steepèd') or somehow drowned and broken ('steepèd and pashed'); or disintegrating in a pulling apart of memory (*dis*remembering) and of self (*dis*membering), not accidentally but in a kind of 'undoing'.

> Fíre-féaturing heaven. For earth | her being has unbound,
>   her dapple is at end, as-
> Tray or aswarm, all throughther, in throngs; | self ín self
>   steepèd and pashed—qúite
> Disremembering, dísmembering | àll now. Heart, you round
>   me right
> With: Óur évening is over us; óur night | whélms, whélms,
>   ánd will end us.

By the end of the sonnet's first eight lines, evening has given way to time's doubly overwhelming night; then the sonnet turns into the final six lines and a new vista, a new fragmentation emerges. Language becomes sharp and fractured, with 'beak-leaved boughs', 'dragonish' in the 'tool-smooth bleak light'; and words echo and emphasize each other ('beak', 'bleak'). Now a once-dappled world unwinds across the words and life's 'once skéined stained véined variety' finds itself on 'two spools'. Now there are 'two flocks, two folds – black, white; | right, wrong':

>   Lét life, wáned,
>   ah lét life wind
> Off hér once skéined stained véined varíety | upon, áll on
>   twó spools; párt, pen, páck
> Now her áll in twó flocks, twó folds—black, white; | right,
>   wrong; ...

As the 'right, wrong' of the 'two flocks, two folds' suggest, there is no easy comfort towards the end of 'Spelt from Sibyl's Leaves'. The poem takes us into a world beyond our imagining: one in which all that we are and all that has been is brought to judgement. Yet, perhaps as much as the black-and-white of a judged world, we hear how dark and light 'tell, each off the other' as if in a relationship – as with the light and dark we all carry and that we bring before God. We know the challenge of this; Hopkins knew the intensity of a self laid bare to its own thoughts and terrors:

> Where, selfwrung, selfstrung, sheathe- and shelterless, |
> thóughts agaínst thoughts ín groans grínd.

Maundy Thursday is a night of such terrors: a night of betrayal and love where 'thóughts agaínst thoughts ín groans grínd' for those at the heart of its deepest tragedy, and where the self-confronts itself. If we have felt called in Lent to travel to the depths of ourselves and discover who we are before God, we are not alone. We are in the company of One who knew the deepest Gethsemane-terrors of confronting darkness and entered that place where all confrontations are held and known. We are in the company of One who holds us, knows tears and mourning and cries out to God in the deepest of suffering: 'My Father, if it is possible, let this cup pass from me; yet not what I want but what you want.'[107]

Day 39

Good Friday

The times are nightfall, look, their light grows less

The times are nightfall, look, their light grows less;
The times are winter, watch, a world undone:
They waste, they wither worse; they as they run
Or bring more or more blazon man's distress.
And I not help. Nor word now of success:
All is from wreck, here, there, to rescue one—
Work which to see scarce so much as begun
Makes welcome death, does dear forgetfulness.
Or what is else? There is your world within.
There rid the dragons, root out there the sin.
Your will is law in that small commonweal.

It was now about noon, and darkness came over the whole land until three in the afternoon, while the sun's light failed; and the curtain of the temple was torn in two. Then Jesus, crying with a loud voice, said, 'Father, into your hands I commend my spirit.' Having said this, he breathed his last. (Luke 23.44–46)

The darkness of Good Friday is with us; and this undone time of nightfall-in-daytime draws us closer to the pull and purpose of the Passion, and into a darkness that covers all things and challenges all things. Hopkins' 'The times are nightfall' – this gentle and curiously chilly not-quite-sonnet – also invites us into a place of darkness at a time of darkness.

Living in Dublin as Professor of Greek and Examiner in

Classics when he wrote this poem, Hopkins' own 'nightfall' was a blend of isolation and alienation, overwork and disquiet about the path his order was taking. These, and the swirling political landscape of Ireland, led him to times of deep desolation. 'Oh my God, look down on me,'[108] he wrote in an impassioned plea towards the end of his Dublin years, shortly before his unique poetic voice fell silent.

Written in the same season of his life as 'Spelt from Sibyl's Leaves' and the 'Terrible Sonnets', 'The times are nightfall' has an elegant precision so different from the flourishes of some of his earlier poetry; it paints the troubles of the world with meaning-filled brevity. There is an urgency to its tone, with emphatic clipped stresses on words carrying the sense of the dark seeming to chase the light away ('times', 'night', 'look', 'light', 'less'). It is as if, in a profound echo of our own times, we are being called to bear witness ('look', 'watch') to the times and their sorrows, as the light seems to decrease and cold creeps across our 'undone' world:

> The times are nightfall, look, their light grows less;
> The times are winter, watch, a world undone:
> They waste, they wither worse; they as they run
> Or bring more or more blazon man's distress.

After the call to look and watch, Hopkins shifts our attention slightly to how 'the times' 'waste' and 'wither worse'. Whether this suggests that 'the times' are themselves wasting and withering or they *lay* waste and *cause* withering, 'the times' now themselves seem more active in ushering in nightfall. In a repetition more breathless than if Hopkins had written 'they run and run,' we hear 'they as they run', as if the times are rushing to flaunt, to 'blazon man's distress'.

> And I not help. Nor word now of success:
> All is from wreck, here, there, to rescue one—
> Work which to see scarce so much as begun
> Makes welcome death, does dear forgetfulness.

DAY 39: GOOD FRIDAY

'And I not help,' says the poet, in fragmentary, condensed and barely held together words, which express the helplessness of one unable to help or of one who is *not* themselves helped. Words just as condensed tumble through the next few lines, in a kind of jagged lament of a writer struggling to write and in the paradox of a poet of unique creativity crafting a picture of his own wordless struggle. 'Nor word now of success,' he says, using this strange word for a poet-priest; it may nevertheless hint at his sense of what might have been, at words that will not come or dreams for the future lost in these nightfall times, opening up a vision of death and 'dear forgetfulness'.

When the sonnet turns again, we are offered the merest possibility of a hope. The language falls into a more regular, less disjointed pattern: the sounds lengthen and breath comes more easily in the reading of lines that speak to – whom? They may be spoken to God, who – even in the depths of nightfall – holds our 'world within' and frees us of our 'dragons': the heart's serpents. 'Your will', the poet might be saying to God, 'is law in that small commonweal'. The heart, our inner world, is God's kingdom even if the times are nightfall. Or perhaps these lines are spoken to us. If so, Hopkins may be inviting us to attend to our own 'world within', where – even in the 'nightfall' of the times – we can 'root out there the sin'. We can at least attend to hearts that faint, lose courage or allow themselves to become separated from the love of God to overcome the 'dragons' at the heart's door. In these final lines of what may be a fragment, it seems that we are invited to discover God and ourselves in our 'world within'; to discover a blend of grace and agency, which – even in the bleakest of times, even in the deepest of nightfalls – may craft and shape a heart given to God.

> Or what is else? There is your world within.
> There rid the dragons, root out there the sin.
> Your will is law in that small commonweal.

How this apparent fragment would have ended if the sestet had been completed is impossible to know, as is why Hopkins might have left it unfinished. It may be that his slight turn towards hope felt too suddenly optimistic after the earlier darkness; or the encouragement to 'rid the dragons' felt too simple a response to a sense of powerlessness. Perhaps 'The times are nightfall' was a fragment born of waiting, of staying in the dark until hope and grace had forged and crafted a heart strengthened for the nightfall times. Perhaps this is a fragment for the nightfall-in-daytime of Good Friday, in which all our bruises, all our sorrows, all our darkness and even a desire for 'dear forgetfulness' are held by the One who embraces these nightfall times on our behalf: the One with whom we reach towards newness of life.

One of the criminals who were hanged there kept deriding him and saying, 'Are you not the Messiah? Save yourself and us!' But the other rebuked him, saying, 'Do you not fear God, since you are under the same sentence of condemnation? And we indeed have been condemned justly, for we are getting what we deserve for our deeds, but this man has done nothing wrong.' Then he said, 'Jesus, remember me when you come into your kingdom.' He replied, 'Truly I tell you, today you will be with me in Paradise.' (Luke 23.39–43)

Day 40

Holy Saturday

That Nature Is a Heraclitean Fire and of the Comfort of the Resurrection

Cloud-puffball, torn tufts, tossed pillows | flaunt forth, then chevy on an air-
Built thoroughfare: heaven-roysterers, in gay-gangs | they throng; they glitter in marches.
Down roughcast, down dazzling whitewash, | wherever an elm arches,
Shivelights and shadowtackle ín long | lashes lace, lance, and pair.
Delightfully the bright wind boisterous | ropes, wrestles, beats earth bare
Of yestertempest's creases; | in pool and rut peel parches
Squandering ooze to squeezed | dough, crust, dust; stanches, starches
Squadroned masks and manmarks | treadmire toil there
Footfretted in it. Million-fuelèd, | nature's bonfire burns on.
But quench her bonniest, dearest | to her, her clearest-selvèd spark
Man, how fast his firedint, | his mark on mind, is gone!
Both are in an unfathomable, all is in an enormous dark
Drowned. O pity and indig | nation! Manshape, that shone
Sheer off, disseveral, a star, | death blots black out; nor mark
                Is any of him at all so stark
But vastness blurs and time | beats level. Enough! the Resurrection,

A heart's-clarion! Away grief's gasping, | joyless days,
  dejection.
                    Across my foundering deck shone
A beacon, an eternal beam. | Flesh fade, and mortal trash
Fall to the residuary worm; | world's wildfire, leave but ash:
              In a flash, at a trumpet crash,
I am all at once what Christ is, | since he was what I am, and
This Jack, joke, poor potsherd, | patch, matchwood,
  immortal diamond,
              Is immortal diamond.

How long and how short these days of Holy Week as we progress towards the Passion. How far we have travelled on this Lenten journey of light and shadows. On Holy Saturday, we remain in the shadows; but arcing towards sunset, we may discover the first intimations of an Easter Dawn not quite on the horizon: one foreshadowed in a nighttime bonfire, flames licking into the dark of the nightfall times and beak-leaved boughs of recent days. And the turn towards resurrection may stir within us: Easter People, who live in the knowledge of what has been suffered and what has been redeemed.

Written just a year before his death, Hopkins' majestic, late poem 'That Nature Is a Heraclitean Fire and of the Comfort of the Resurrection' brings us full circle in this dappled season. Glory be to God for dappled things, we heard 40 days ago. And here we discover again the dappling of God's world in ever-changing nature, in life lost and found, and in humanity's spark: all in this most sublime expression of pied beauty. Freshly forged phrases, repetitions, echoes and meanings chase across the page to express how 'Nature Is a Heraclitean Fire': that is, to express the idea (emerging from the pre-Socratic philosopher Heraclitus) that nature endlessly churns and changes, with the glow and spark of fire as its guiding symbol and its most fundamental, transformational element.

The poem begins with the scudding flux and movement of soft billowing clouds as they chase across the sky – a flurry of fast sounds as round and gentle as the clouds they figure forth:

DAY 40: HOLY SATURDAY

> Cloud-puffball, torn tufts, tossed pillows | flaunt forth, then chevy on an air-
> Built thoroughfare: heaven-roysterers, in gay-gangs | they throng; they glitter in marches.
> Down roughcast, down dazzling whitewash, | wherever an elm arches,
> Shivelights and shadowtackle ín long | lashes lace, lance, and pair.

These 'puffball', 'torn tufts' clouds tumble along their way, playing boisterously as they 'throng' and 'glitter' across the skies. Away from the revelling clouds, we are shown more flux in the interplay of light and dark: a magic lantern show of light piercing through arched tree branches ('shivelights') and in the chiaroscuro of branches ('shadowtackle') reaching dark tendrils into the night.

The flux of nature goes on: exuberant wind wrangles the damp earth, beating it 'bare of yestertempest's creases'. This bouncing, rhythmic and evocative compound word brings before us the scars – the 'creases' – of previous storms and, at the same time, banishes them from our vision, so rapid is the flux of nature. The clouds and storms pass, and now the earth dries:

> | in pool and rut peel parches
> Squandering ooze to squeezed | dough, crust, dust; stanches, starches
> Squadroned masks and manmarks | treadmire toil there
> Footfretted in it. Million-fuelèd, | nature's bonfire burns on.

Pool turns to rutted earth and parched ground, its moisture ('ooze') lost. And through travelling, repeated sounds, all turns to 'squeezed dough' and then to 'crust' and 'dust'. In just a few words, pool has turned to dust, capturing the imprints of humanity ('manmarks') in the ancient 'footfretted' earth. Still 'nature's bonfire [the churn and flux and transformations of life; its beginnings and its endings] burns on'. In the midst of this, humankind is nature's greatest triumph: its most beloved, 'bonniest, dearest ... clearest-selvèd spark' burning brightly at the heart of endless change and transformation. Yet if all things change, if all earth turns to dust and crust, so too must we be lost to the world ('quench[ed]'), even though our 'firedint' (the mark we leave in the fire of nature) seems to be 'fast' (embedded in the world). Our mark – our spark – is drowned in darkness and our 'manshape', the shape of our humanity, is scattered.

                                      Manshape, that shone
Sheer off, disseveral, a star, | death blots black out; nor mark
                Is any of him at all so stark
But vastness blurs and time | beats level.

The fiery churn of nature seems unquenchable; but then the poem shifts, and time shifts, and we are no longer caught in the endless churn of Heraclitean fire. In a kind of volta, a greater transformation breaks through the poet's vision and into ours. 'Enough!' the poet exclaims and, as if with a strike of the fist or a shake of the head, he tries to dispel the mesmerizing endless timebound cycle to discover something that radically cuts through and shapes time:

                            Enough! the Resurrection,
A heart's-clarion! Away grief's gasping, | joyless days,
   dejection.
                Across my foundering deck shone
A beacon, an eternal beam.

'Enough! the Resurrection': this moment, this herald of something new in the world's labours, is with us today as Holy Saturday speaks to us of resurrection, which is personal and more than personal; which enters into and reaches beyond time. Now, far from the sublime but impersonal churn of the world's transformations, and far from the guttering of myriad sparks, Hopkins catches us up in his passionate response to his Saviour. 'A heart's-clarion!' he cries as the Resurrection calls.

DAY 40: HOLY SATURDAY

'Away grief's gasping,' we hear, in sounds that echo the faltering of breath; away 'joyless days'. Across '*my* foundering deck', says Hopkins, discovering himself within the Resurrection story, 'shone / A beacon, an eternal beam': this is resurrection that is personal, eternal and passionate.

Though our flesh will fade and feed the 'residuary worm' and though ashes will remain, recalling the beginning of this season, this is nothing to the 'flash, at a trumpet crash' of the Resurrection we taste at Easter. Biblical echoes shimmer through these lines: Christ will return with 'a cry of command' and 'the sound of God's trumpet';[109] and in the dawning of Easter, he will be the 'first fruits of those who have died'.[110] In the bright, sudden clamour of God-with-us, 'all at once' we are transformed by the one who has been with us as one of us; so we are utterly caught up in the transforming love of God:

> I am all at once what Christ is, | since he was what I am, and
> This Jack, joke, poor potsherd, | patch, matchwood,
>   immortal diamond,
>   Is immortal diamond.

The transformation of resurrection takes us far beyond the churn and flux of the Heraclitean fire: it takes us into our identity in and with Christ. 'He was what I am,' Hopkins says and – having travelled through a sound-smudge of our 'Jack, joke, | poor potsherd, / patch, matchwood' ordinariness – he declares: 'immortal diamond, / Is immortal diamond.' We are caught up in the humanity of Christ and in the immortal diamond of our gifted identity: fire, earth, transmutation, transformation, timeless beauty, depth and spark. Immortal diamond.

Day 41

Easter Day

The Wreck of the Deutschland

Part 3, Stanzas 32–5

> I admire thee, master of the tides,
>   Of the Yore-flood, of the year's fall;
>   The recurb and the recovery of the gulf's sides,
>   The girth of it and the wharf of it and the wall;
> Staunching, quenching ocean of a motionable mind;
> Ground of being, and granite of it: past all
>   Grasp God, throned behind
> Death with a sovereignty that heeds but hides, bodes but abides;
>
>   With a mercy that outrides
>   The all of water, an ark
>   For the listener; for the lingerer with a love glides
>   Lower than death and the dark;
> A vein for the visiting of the past-prayer, pent in prison,
> The-last-breath penitent spirits—the uttermost mark
>   Our passion-plungèd giant risen,
> The Christ of the Father compassionate, fetched in the storm of his strides.
>
>   Now burn, new born to the world,
>   Doubled-naturèd name,
>   The heaven-flung, heart-fleshed, maiden-furled
>   Miracle-in-Mary-of-flame,

DAY 41: EASTER DAY

> Mid-numbered he in three of the thunder-throne!
> Not a dooms-day dazzle in his coming nor dark as he came;
>   Kind, but royally reclaiming his own;
> A released shower, let flash to the shire, not a lightning of
> fíre hard-hurled.
>
>   Dame, at our door
>   Drowned, and among our shoals,
>   Remember us in the roads, the heaven-haven of the
>   Reward:
>   Our Kíng back, Oh, upon énglish sóuls!
> Let him easter in us, be a dayspring to the dimness of us,
>   be a crimson-cresseted east,
>   More brightening her, rare-dear Britain, as his reign rolls,
>   Pride, rose, prince, hero of us, high-priest,
> Our hearts' charity's hearth's fire, our thoughts' chivalry's
> throng's Lord.

'Let him easter in us, be a dayspring to the dimness of us.'

The passion of the storm that sank the *Deutschland* abated. So affected was Hopkins by pathos and the mystery of the sisters lost in the wreckage, as they travelled towards religious freedom, that the poetic gift he had thought did 'not belong ... to his profession'[111] was resurrected.

At the heart of the storm, the physical presence of one of the sisters commanded the scene; and this 'lioness', this 'prophetess' as Hopkins describes her elsewhere in 'The Wreck',[112] became for him a vision of courageous, accepting, surrendered faith. As he lay safely 'in the loveable west', 'under a roof' and 'at rest', he said, she was calling, 'O Christ, Christ, come quickly' as her own cross approached. 'She calls Christ to her,' said Hopkins, and so 'christens her wild-worst Best':[113] tragedy and grace are blended, even to her life's 'christened' end.

Now, in these final verses, the poem draws us back towards Christ. It pulls us back to the mercy, mastery and mystery (or 'incomprehensible certainty'[114]) of God, who lies behind and within the waves and who sustains us and draws us on through life's grace and drownings and resurrections. 'I admire thee, master of the tides,' Hopkins begins these final verses, as he pours before us God as container, restrainer and mover of the waters. This is God whose mastery holds in place – 'recurbs' – the sea's immensity: the whole *'girth* of it and the *wharf* of it and the *wall'*, Hopkins stresses, as the unfathomable power and fluidity of our creator God – the 'staunching, quenching ocean of a motionable mind' – flows through the verse.

Now though, God is our foundation as well as our flow, the

> Ground of being, and granite of it: past all
>   Grasp God, throned behind
> Death with a sovereignty that heeds but hides, bodes but abides;

Our beyond-all-understanding God rules even death, and 'heeds but hides, bodes but abides'. He may seem hidden by death but he observes and knows all things; and even in tragedy, God always 'abides'. His is a mercy, we hear in stanza 33, that 'outrides / The all of water', defying our overwhelmings and reaching even those who are

>   past-prayer, pent in prison,
> The-last-breath penitent spirits.

As the stanza goes on, Christ, our 'passion-plungèd giant risen', our fallen and resurrected Saviour, pounds through the verse in sounds that gather emphasis as they echo and build:

> Our passion-plungèd giant risen,
> The Christ of the Father compassionate, fetched in the
>   storm of his strides.

'Passion' and 'compassion' echo each other to draw out the depth of a love – the self-emptying strength of a love – that brought God among us in Christ, roaring through the world 'in the storm of his strides'. The intensity of this vision of Christ only deepens as the poem draws towards its end, as if in

DAY 41: EASTER DAY

a final flurry and passion of a storm. And in a tumbling series of compound words, we hear the poet's cry:

> Now burn, new born to the world,
>   Doubled-naturèd name,
> The heaven-flung, heart-fleshed, maiden-furled
>   Miracle-in-Mary-of-flame,
> Mid-numbered he in three of the thunder-throne!

It is as if Hopkins appeals to Christ made newly present and carried ('new born' rather than 'newborn') in the fresh tragedy of the wreck. Here, the compassion and mercy of the 'Miracle-in-Mary-of-flame' burn brightly; and with layered sounds and carefully swaddled thoughts (Jesus is 'maiden-furled': wrapped in his mother), Hopkins brings before us the Incarnate One, 'Mid-numbered he in three', come to reclaim 'his own'.

Whether, for Hopkins, 'his own' are all Christian souls or souls inspired by the faith of the lost 'dame' to whom he appeals for intercession, the final verse leads us towards a heartfelt plea for resurrection for his homeland, where the *Deutschland* was lost in terror and darkness. Beyond the storms, pleads Hopkins,

> Let him easter in us, be a dayspring to the dimness of us,
>   be a crimson-cresseted east,
> More brightening her, rare-dear Britain, as his reign rolls,
>   Pride, rose, prince, hero of us, high-priest,
> Our hearts' charity's hearth's fire, our thoughts' chivalry's
>   throng's Lord.

'Let him easter in us,' says Hopkins: let the one who has lived and died in life's storms and drownings become our brightness, a 'dayspring to the dimness of us', as the sun rises in the 'crimson-cresseted east'.

'Let him easter in us': let Christ, who weaves through our ordinary, mixed life, bring us to new life even after the darkest passion-tide; even after we have been all but overwhelmed by the storm.

'Let him easter in us.'

Notes

1 A. H. Miles, ed., 1891, *The Poets and Poetry of the Century: Robert Bridges and Contemporary Poets*, London: Hutchinson & Co., p. 162.
2 Claude Colleer Abbott, ed., 1955, *The Letters of Gerard Manley Hopkins to Robert Bridges*, 2nd edn, London: Oxford University Press, pp. 135, 159.
3 Colleer Abbott, *Letters of Gerard Manley Hopkins*, p. 246.
4 Hopkins, 'Notes on the Spiritual Exercises, 7 Aug 1882', in Catherine Phillips, ed., 2009, *Gerard Manley Hopkins: The Major Works, including All the Poems and Selected Prose*, Oxford: Oxford University Press, p. 282.
5 For more on instress and inscape, see Day 20 Thursday: 'As Kingfishers Catch Fire'.
6 The curtal sonnet is explored in more detail in Day 3 Friday: 'Peace'.
7 Colleer Abbott, *Letters of Gerard Manley Hopkins*, p. 183.
8 Lois W. Pitchford, 'The Curtal Sonnets of Gerard Manley Hopkins', *Modern Language Notes*, 67, no. 3, 1952, p. 166.
9 That is, Alexandrines, which comprise 12 syllables in each line, usually with a break after the sixth syllable.
10 J. Malpas, ed., 2007, *Clwydian Range: Area of Outstanding Natural Beauty (AONB) – Local Geodiversity Action Plan (LGAP)*.
11 Jürgen Moltmann, 1967, *The Theology of Hope*, trans. James W. Leitch, London: SCM Press, p. 25.
12 Rowan Williams, 2016, *Being Disciples: Essentials of the Christian Life*, London: SPCK Publishing, Kindle Edition, p. 29.
13 Moltmann, *Theology of Hope*, p. 25.
14 Williams, *Being Disciples*, p. 29.
15 1 Corinthians 13.12.
16 Alongside 'Carrion Comfort', they are considered to include 'To Seem the Stranger', 'I Wake and Feel', 'No Worst', 'Patience, Hard Thing' and 'My own heart let me more have pity on'. Robert Bridges referred to Hopkins' 'Terrible Sonnets' on p. 101 of his

edition of his friend's poetry, published in 1918: *Poems of Gerard Manley Hopkins*, London: Humphrey Milford.
17   Colleer Abbott, *Letters of Gerard Manley Hopkins*, p. 221.
18   The many scriptural references to God's leonine power include Job 10.16, Isaiah 31.4, Hosea 11.10 and Revelation 5.5.
19   There are echoes of Psalm 22.1 and Matthew 27.46.
20   The title is inspired by George Herbert's poem 'The Size', which ends 'These seas are tears, and heav'n the haven.'
21   See John 7.37–38.
22   Paul Mariani, 2008, *Gerard Manley Hopkins: A Life*, London: Penguin, Kindle Edition, pp. 180–2.
23   The sestet follows the unusual scheme of 'cdcdcd'.
24   Colleer Abbott, *Letters of Gerard Manley Hopkins*, p. 84.
25   Matthew 7.3. In the Douay Rheims translation of the Latin Vulgate Bible into English, the verse says: 'And why seest thou the mote that is in thy brother's eye; and seest not the beam that is in thy own eye.'
26   The Met Office Digital Library and Archive, *Ten-Year Rainfall 1870–79*.
27   Mariani, *Gerard Manley Hopkins*, p. 167.
28   Claude Colleer Abbott, ed., 1955, *The Correspondence of Gerard Manley Hopkins and Richard Watson Dixon*, 2nd edn, London: Oxford University Press, p. 14.
29   Colleer Abbott, *Correspondence of Gerard Manley Hopkins*, p. 14.
30   Colleer Abbott, *Letters of Gerard Manley Hopkins*, p. 168.
31   Mariani, *Gerard Manley Hopkins*, p. 173.
32   In a postcard to Robert Bridges, he said: 'The kind people of the sonnet were the Watsons of Shooter's Hill, nothing to do with the Elwy.' Colleer Abbott, *Letters of Gerard Manley Hopkins*, p. 76.
33   See the reflection in Day 6 Tuesday: 'Carrion Comfort' for more about Hopkins' 'Terrible Sonnets' or 'Sonnets of Desolation'.
34   Colleer Abbott, *Letters of Gerard Manley Hopkins*, pp. 216, 221.
35   Colleer Abbott, *Letters of Gerard Manley Hopkins*, p. 221.
36   Colleer Abbott, *Letters of Gerard Manley Hopkins*, p. 219.
37   Colleer Abbott, *Letters of Gerard Manley Hopkins*, p. 218.
38   M. Andrew and R. Waldon, eds, 1978, *The Poems of the 'Pearl' Manuscript: 'Pearl', 'Cleanness', 'Patience', 'Sir Gawain and the Green Knight'*, York Medieval Texts, 2nd Series, London: Edward Arnold.
39   Colleer Abbott, *Letters of Gerard Manley Hopkins*, p. 221.
40   Louis J. Puhl, trans. and ed., 2021, *The Spiritual Exercises of St Ignatius of Loyola*, 2nd edn, Chicago: Loyola Press, Kindle Edition.
41   Colleer Abbott, *Letters of Gerard Manley Hopkins*, p. 221.

NOTES

42 'To Seem the Stranger' and 'I Wake and Feel' sit opposite 'Patience, Hard Thing' and 'My own heart let me more have pity on'.
43 Colleer Abbott, *Letters of Gerard Manley Hopkins*, p. 221.
44 Bridges, *Poems of Gerard Manley Hopkins*, p. 119.
45 Met Office Digital Library and Archive, *Daily Weather Reports, 1875*.
46 Psalm 139.13.
47 Colleer Abbott, *Letters of Gerard Manley Hopkins*, pp. 187–8.
48 There is more about sprung rhythm in the reflection in Day 10 Saturday: 'God's Grandeur'.
49 Psalm 34.8.
50 Colleer Abbott, *Letters of Gerard Manley Hopkins*, p. 85.
51 Mariani, *Gerard Manley Hopkins*, p. 177.
52 See Day 10 Saturday: 'God's Grandeur' for more on sprung rhythm.
53 Colleer Abbott, *Correspondence of Gerard Manley Hopkins*, p. 15.
54 Hopkins, 'Notes on the Spiritual Exercises, 7 Aug 1882', in Phillips, *Gerard Manley Hopkins*, p. 282.
55 'Minion' has roots in the Old and Middle French *mignon*, with overtones of a royal favourite or darling.
56 Colleer Abbott, *Letters of Gerard Manley Hopkins*, p. 56.
57 Colleer Abbott, *Correspondence of Gerard Manley Hopkins*, p. 42; *Letters of Gerard Manley Hopkins*, p. 135.
58 Claude Colleer Abbott, ed., 1956, *Further Letters of Gerard Manley Hopkins, including His Correspondence with Coventry Patmore*, 2nd edn, London: Oxford University Press, p. 243.
59 George Orwell wrote this in *The Observer* in November 1944 when reviewing W. H. Gardner's two-volume work, *Gerard Manley Hopkins (1844–1889): A Study of Poetic Idiosyncrasy in Relation to Poetic Tradition*, published in London by Martin Secker & Warburg.
60 Hopkins, in Christopher Devlin SJ, ed., 1959, *The Sermons and Devotional Writings of Gerard Manley Hopkins*, London: Oxford University Press, p. 103.
61 'The Wreck of the Deutschland', line 141.
62 From a sermon preached on the Sunday evening of 23 November 1879, in Phillips, *Gerard Manley Hopkins*, p. 282.
63 Colleer Abbott, *Letters of Gerard Manley Hopkins*, p. 86.
64 Colleer Abbott, *Letters of Gerard Manley Hopkins*, p. 86.
65 Hopkins, 'Notes on the Spiritual Exercises, 20 Aug 1880', in Phillips, *Gerard Manley Hopkins*, p. 282.
66 Hopkins, 'Notes on the Spiritual Exercises, 20 Aug 1880', p. 282.
67 Quoted in Norman White, 1992, *Hopkins: A Literary Biography*, Oxford: Clarendon Press, p. 129.
68 Matthew 6.28.

69 Hopkins, 'Retreat Notes, 1 Jan 1889', in Phillips, *Gerard Manley Hopkins*, pp. 302–3.
70 Hopkins, 'Retreat Notes, 1 Jan 1889', pp. 302–3.
71 Hopkins, 'Retreat Notes, 1 Jan 1889', pp. 303.
72 Martin Dubois, 2019, *Gerard Manley Hopkins and the Poetry of Religious Experience*, Cambridge Studies in Nineteenth-Century Literature and Culture 108, Cambridge: Cambridge University Press, Kindle Edition, p. 45.
73 Colleer Abbott, *Letters of Gerard Manley Hopkins*, p. 104. Hopkins intended for the poem to 'carr[y] the reader along'.
74 Colleer Abbott, *Correspondence of Gerard Manley Hopkins*, p. 149.
75 White, *Hopkins*, p. 461. This poem is sometimes published as unfinished, with some incomplete final lines, which have not been included here.
76 Quoted in White, *Hopkins*, p. 462.
77 Mariani, *Gerard Manley Hopkins*, p. 248.
78 Colleer Abbott, *Correspondence of Gerard Manley Hopkins*, p. 38.
79 See Hopkins' preface in Bridges, *Poems of Gerard Manley Hopkins*, pp. 5–6.
80 Colleer Abbott, *Correspondence of Gerard Manley Hopkins*, p. 26.
81 Colleer Abbott, *Letters of Gerard Manley Hopkins*, p. 158.
82 See reflections in Day 24 Tuesday: 'The Leaden Echo' and Day 25 Wednesday: 'The Golden Echo'.
83 Luke 23.34 and Genesis 3.22–24. This may also recall the words written by John Ball at the time of the Peasants' Revolt in 1381: 'When Adam delved and Eve span, who was then the gentleman?' See Mark O'Brien, 2016, *When Adam Delved and Eve Span: A History of the Peasants' Revolt of 1381*, London: Bookmarks Publications.
84 For example, in 'The Sea and the Skylark'.
85 This echoes a kenning-word used in the Anglo-Saxon poem *Beowulf*.
86 T. S. Eliot, 1944, 'The Dry Salvages', in *The Four Quartets*, London: Faber & Faber.
87 *Tourists' Guide to North Wales: Giving a Full Description of Its Principal Centres for Excursions, etc.*, 1877, Manchester: Abel Heywood and Son, pp. 9–10.
88 Colleer Abbott, *Letters of Gerard Manley Hopkins*, p. 163.
89 Hopkins called this 'vowelling'.
90 Colleer Abbott, *Letters of Gerard Manley Hopkins*, p. 164.
91 From Hopkins' poem 'The May Magnificat'.
92 Hopkins, 'Notes on the Spiritual Exercises, 7 Aug 1882', p. 282.
93 White, *Hopkins*, p. 280.
94 White, *Hopkins*, p. 280.

NOTES

95 Colleer Abbott, *Letters of Gerard Manley Hopkins*, p. 163.
96 Romans 8.19. He wrote this in a letter to Dixon. Colleer Abbott, *Correspondence of Gerard Manley Hopkins*, p. 108.
97 Colleer Abbott, *Correspondence of Gerard Manley Hopkins*, p. 109.
98 See Day 31 Wednesday: 'The Sea and the Skylark' for more about 'vowelling'.
99 Hopkins, 'Retreat Notes, 1 Jan 1889', pp. 303–4.
100 See Luke 12.51–53 and Matthew 10.34.
101 Hopkins, 'Retreat Notes, 1 Jan 1889', p. 302.
102 In Job, the whirlwind is a place both of suffering and the place from which God speaks. See Job 27.20 and 37.9; 38.1 and 40.6.
103 This recalls Jesus' words: 'gather the wheat into my barn' (Matthew 13.30b).
104 Colleer Abbott, *Letters of Gerard Manley Hopkins*, p. 246.
105 Colleer Abbott, *Letters of Gerard Manley Hopkins*, p. 246.
106 Hopkins is drawing from the Cumaean Sibyl of the ancient world. The Cumaean Sibyl was considered a guide to the underworld and, in early Christianity, was blended with Christian prophets.
107 Matthew 26.38–39.
108 Hopkins, 'Retreat Notes, 1 Jan 1889', pp. 303–4.
109 1 Thessalonians 4.16.
110 1 Corinthians 15.20.
111 Colleer Abbott, *Correspondence of Gerard Manley Hopkins*, p. 14.
112 Stanza 17.
113 Stanza 24.
114 Colleer Abbott, *Letters of Gerard Manley Hopkins*, pp. 187–8.

References

Unless stated otherwise, biblical texts are from the New Revised Standard Version: The Holy Bible: New Revised Standard Version Anglicized (NRSVUK) Cross-Reference edition, William Collins, 2018.

Andrew, M., and Waldon, R., eds, 1978, *The Poems of the 'Pearl' Manuscript: 'Pearl', 'Cleanness', 'Patience', 'Sir Gawain and the Green Knight'*, York Medieval Texts, 2nd Series, London: Edward Arnold.
Bosco, Mark, 'Plunging into the Depths: A Catholic Aesthetic of Difference', in Bugliani Cox, Francesca, ed., *The Drama of the Spirit: Essays in Memory of Michael Paul Gallagher SJ*, pp. 23–31, https://www.ignaziana.org/wp-content/uploads/2024/01/Gallagher.pdf, accessed 21.05.2025.
Bridges, Robert, ed., 1918, *Poems of Gerard Manley Hopkins*, London: Humphrey Milford.
Colleer Abbott, Claude, ed., 1955, *The Correspondence of Gerard Manley Hopkins and Richard Watson Dixon*, 2nd edn, London: Oxford University Press.
Colleer Abbott, Claude, ed., 1955, *The Letters of Gerard Manley Hopkins to Robert Bridges*, 2nd edn, London: Oxford University Press.
Colleer Abbott, Claude, ed., 1956, *Further Letters of Gerard Manley Hopkins, including His Correspondence with Coventry Patmore*, 2nd edn, London: Oxford University Press, https://ia802900.us.archive.org/32/items/in.ernet.dli.2015.225486/2015.225486.Further-Letters_text.pdf, accessed 21.05.2025.
Devlin SJ, Christopher, ed., 1959, *The Sermons and Devotional Writings of Gerard Manley Hopkins*, London: Oxford University Press.
Dubois, Martin, 2019, *Gerard Manley Hopkins and the Poetry of Religious Experience*, Cambridge Studies in Nineteenth-Century Literature and Culture 108, Cambridge: Cambridge University Press, Kindle Edition.
Eliot, T. S., 1944, 'The Dry Salvages', in *The Four Quartets*, London: Faber & Faber.
Ellsberg, Margaret R., ed., 2017, *The Gospel in Gerard Manley Hop-*

REFERENCES

kins: *Selections from His Poems, Letters, Journals and Spiritual Writings*, Walden, NY: Plough Publishing House, Kindle Edition.

Endean, Philip, 'The Spirituality of Gerard Manley Hopkins,' *The Hopkins Quarterly*, 8, no. 3 (1981), pp. 107–29, http://www.jstor.org/stable/45240925, accessed 25.10.2022.

Gardner, W. H., ed., 1989, *Poems and Prose of Gerard Manley Hopkins Selected with an Introduction and Notes*, London: Penguin, Kindle Edition.

Malpas, J., ed., 2007, *Clwydian Range: Area of Outstanding Natural Beauty (AONB) – Local Geodiversity Action Plan (LGAP)*, https://www.denbighshirecountryside.org.uk/files/LGAP_Report_ENGLISH.pdf, accessed 20.08.2024.

Mariani, Paul, 2008, *Gerard Manley Hopkins: A Life*, London: Penguin, Kindle Edition.

Met Office Digital Library and Archive, *Daily Weather Reports, 1875*, https://digital.nmla.metoffice.gov.uk/IO_5ce5c7fb-1093-4844-adb3-beb5a44e393e/, accessed 11.04.2024.

Met Office Digital Library and Archive, *Ten Year Rainfall 1870_79*, https://digital.nmla.metoffice.gov.uk/SO_4d9f2054-2b3c-4b8d-a1a0-5d0773e32cf7/?pg=2, accessed 20.08.2024.

Miles, A. H., ed., 1891, *The Poets and Poetry of the Century: Robert Bridges and Contemporary Poets*, London: Hutchinson & Co., Internet Archive, University of Toronto, https://archive.org/details/poetsandpoetryof08mileuoft/page/162/mode/1up, accessed 01.02.2025.

Moltmann, Jürgen, 1967, *The Theology of Hope*, trans. James W. Leitch, London: SCM Press.

National Archives, *Post Office: Inland Mails Organisation and Circulation: Records*, https://discovery.nationalarchives.gov.uk/details/r/C11745#:~:text=The%20Dead%20Letter%20Office%20was,and%20collect%20the%20postage%20due, accessed 09.03.2024.

Nixon, Jude V., '"Sweet especial rural scene": Revisiting Binsey', *The Hopkins Quarterly*, 16, no. 1/2 (1989), pp. 39–60, http://www.jstor.org/stable/45241158, accessed 26.01.2025.

Nixon, Jude V., '"vital candle in close heart's vault": Energy, Optics and Hopkins' Spermaceti Flame', *The Hopkins Quarterly*, 32, no. 3/4 (2005), pp. 139–65, http://www.jstor.org/stable/45241498, accessed 05.02.2023.

O'Brien, Mark, 2016, *When Adam Delved and Eve Span: A History of the Peasants' Revolt of 1381*, London: Bookmarks Publications.

Ong, Walter, 1980, *Hopkins, the Self, and God*, Toronto: University of Toronto Press.

Phillips, Catherine, ed., 2009, *Gerard Manley Hopkins: The Major Works, including All the Poems and Selected Prose*, Oxford: Oxford University Press.

Pitchford, Lois W., 'The Curtal Sonnets of Gerard Manley Hopkins', *Modern Language Notes*, 67, no. 3, 1952, pp. 165–9, https://doi.org/10.2307/2909772, accessed 26.09.2023.

Puhl, Louis J., trans. and ed., 2021, *The Spiritual Exercises of St Ignatius of Loyola*, 2nd edn, Chicago: Loyola Press, Kindle Edition.

Randall, Catherine, 2020, *A Heart Lost in Wonder: The Life and Faith of Gerard Manley Hopkins*, Grand Rapids, MI: Eerdmans.

Tourists' Guide to North Wales: Giving a Full Description of Its Principal Centres for Excursions, etc., 1877, Manchester: Abel Heywood and Son, https://books.google.co.uk/books?id=erUHAAAAQAAJ&printsec=frontcover&source=gbs_ge_summary_r&cad=0#v=onepage&q&f=false, accessed 15.06.2024.

Vendler, Helen, 1995, *The Breaking of Style: Hopkins, Heaney, Graham*, The Richard Ellmann Lectures in Modern Literature, Cambridge, MA: Harvard University Press.

Watson, J. R., 1987, *The Poetry of Gerard Manley Hopkins*, Penguin Critical Studies, London: Penguin.

White, Norman, 1992, *Hopkins: A Literary Biography*, Oxford: Clarendon Press.

Williams, Rowan, 2016, *Being Disciples: Essentials of the Christian life*, London: SPCK Publishing, Kindle Edition.

www.ingramcontent.com/pod-product-compliance
Lightning Source LLC
LaVergne TN
LVHW041634060526
838200LV00040B/1569